S.O.S.
The Meaning of Our Crisis

S.O.S.
The Meaning of Our Crisis

by
Aleksandrovich
Pitirim A. Sorokin, *1889–*

51-14377

BOSTON · THE BEACON PRESS

Printed in U. S. A.

To the memory of a dear friend,
Sergei Alexandrovitch Koussevitzky

Contents

Preface

THE YEARS THAT HAVE ELAPSED since the publication of my *Social and Cultural Dynamics*[1] and the *Crisis of Our Age*[2] have confirmed all the essential forecastings made in these volumes. The majestic tragedy of historical processes has been unfolding according to the schedule clearly delineated in *Dynamics* and *Crisis*. Not a single important point in these works has been repudiated by history; not a single basic proposition, therefore, needs drastic revision. What is needed now is a comprehensive outline of the main development of the crisis of our age from 1940 up to the present moment. These essays attempt to perform this task. They depict the main trends of the crisis for this latest period. This function is discharged, however, not in the form of a descriptive enumeration of countless events of the decade considered, but, more fruitfully, by embracing most of the important changes in the formulas of murderous trend, polarization, and totalitarianism. This procedure allows one to depict the main trends more economically, more precisely, and more meaningfully than any descriptive enumeration can do. In addition, it acquaints the readers with the uniformities of polarization and totalitarianism, still little known to the public at large as well as to the social scientists.

---

[1] Four volumes, New York, 1937-41.

[2] New York, 1941. Appeared since in Portuguese (1945), Czech (1948), Norwegian (1948), Spanish (1948), German (1950), Dutch (1950), and Japanese (1951) translations, and is being translated into Finnish, French, and Russian.

The main trend of the decade 1941-1951 has consisted of an unfolding and maturing of the crisis. The reality of the crisis itself and its basic nature have now become incomparably clearer than they were before 1937 (the year of publication of three volumes of my *Dynamics*). In that earlier period its visibility was so low that the overwhelming majority of people and their leaders simply did not see it. Therefore they categorically denied its existence, confidently believing in streamlined progress. After 1939, the crisis developed so tragically fast, its devastations became so apocalyptic, its victims numbered so many millions and their grotesque corpses were scattered over so wide an area, that its terrible reality is now experienced by everyone; its awe-inspiring majesty is visible to all; and its deadening thunder fills the whole human universe. The crisis has come of age.

The subsequent studies deal with the central trends of the crisis; the first three give a portraiture of the murderous and destructive trend of the crisis, as it developed after 1939; the fourth supplies an analysis and the formula of the trend of polarization; the fifth furnishes a formula for the causes and fluctuations of totalitarianism.

In depicting the destructive trend, I intentionally abandon dry, scientific description in favor of a dramatic, impressionistic-expressionistic portraiture. The very nature of the trend, and the great examples of Erasmus's *The Praise of Folly*, T. Carlyle's *Sartor Resartus* or F. Nietzsche's *Also Sprach Zarathustra* justify this preference. No apology is made for this indulgence.

Rise and decline of governmental regimentation and polarization in the individuals and groups are two basic processes recurring again and again in all societies and periods. They are going on full blast at the present time. They tangibly influence our lives, activities, and happiness. They are daily talked about by housewives, discussed by politicians, studied by scholars, treated by psychiatrists, damned by some, glorified by others. And yet their real nature and especially their causes and uniformities remain little known, not only to the rank and file but even to social scientists, statesmen, business and labor leaders.

These essays aim to throw a light on these dark problems. Among other things the essays formulate a few causal laws about these processes. However approximate, these formulas of uniformities are possibly among the very small number of roughly valid "social laws" discovered by the social and psychological sciences. An understanding of the real causes of rise and decline of totalitarianism makes superfluous, even stupid, most of the heated arguments and bloody wars between the partisans of Communism and capitalism, totalitarianism and democracy. For an elimination of totalitarianism, the knowledge of the "law of fluctuation of totalitarianism" dictates policies quite different from those pursued at the present time by the partisans of free society. The same is true of the law of polarization. Grasp of it helps us comprehend a host of events daily happening around us and with ourselves. Its understanding suggests therapies different from the prevalent ones against the mental, moral, and social evils of the polarized humanity of our age.

In conclusion, I wish to thank the Lilly Endowment, Inc., and Mr. Eli Lilly for financial help in the preparation of these essays.

PITIRIM A. SOROKIN

Harvard University

S.O.S.

The Meaning of Our Crisis

CHAPTER ONE

S.O.S.

ALL-MERCIFUL GOD! Save our souls from ourselves! Man the Killer is again at large. "The worst of the beasts" once more prowls on this planet, more insane than ever before, more destructive than the greatest earthquake, more cunning than the devil. Carefully polished, scientific up to his fingertips, brotherly-humanitarian in his civilized looks, big-hearted in his highfalutin talks, Man the Killer has become the Death of Man's body; the Death of Man's Spirit; the Death of Man's Culture; and the Death of Man's beautiful dreams.

"Thou shalt not kill" is rejected by him as a subversive pacifism. "Love thine enemy" is prosecuted as high treason. "Operation Killer" is glorified as the sublimest heroism. Man the Creator is suppressed and Man the Peacemaker is silenced. Man the Destroyer reigns supreme. He is the new all-mighty God. . . .

He kills my Korean and American brothers. He murders my Russian and English brothers. He exterminates my Chinese and Hindu, my German and French brothers. He destroys all my brothers, in all nations, everywhere.

He rapes all my sisters: European and Asiatic, American and African, Australian and Indonesian.

By atom bombs he atomizes my fathers. By rockets he pierces the hearts of my mothers. By phosphorous bombs he burns

3

to death my grandparents. By gas-jellied bombs he tortures to death my baby grandchildren. Mercilessly he bombards, shoots, explodes, strangles, drowns, crushes, suffocates, radioactivates, poisons, burns, infects, torpedoes, starves, freezes all human beings and all living creatures, in the sky, on the earth, and under the water. He is everywhere. And there is no place to be safe from him.

He never kills as tigers kill: without big words and justification. He calls his murders "Heroic Crusades," crusades in the name of God or Humanity, Religion or Atheism, Communism or Capitalism, Autocracy or Democracy, Freedom or Peace, "My Country" or "Our Way of Life," Idealism or Materialism, Labor or Management, Aristocracy or Proletariat, Revolution or Reaction, Progress or Order, "Chosen People," Justice or Equality, or other big words — all empty and dead. And the hollower the word the bloodier the Crusade.

In this century his favorite Crusades have been for the sake of *"Deutschland über alles,"* "To make the world safe for democracy," "Communism and Dictatorship of the Proletariat," "Capitalism and Free Enterprise," "Fascism" and "Four Freedoms," "Liberation from Something or Nothing," "Atheism" and "Religion," "War To End All Wars" and "Peace," "Revolution" and "Counter-Revolution," "Preservation of Civilization and Culture" and "War for no reason at all."

For the sake of these words the Killer of our age murdered, mutilated, and doomed to death many millions of human beings in the awe-inspiring Crusade of the Chinese revolution going strong since 1911; some twenty-five million in the "sacred" Crusade of the First World War; about thirty million in the "glorious" Russian revolution; some sixty million in the "holy" Crusade of the Second World War.

Now, after these great killings, the Destroyer rests. Resting, he prepares the plans for his last judgement — the death for this planet and its inhabitants. In between, he amuses himself by various "police actions" in Korea and Indo-China, the Dutch Indies and the Middle East, in Greece and elsewhere. This game has already ruined a country of thirty million. It has killed, mutilated, and doomed to extinction some two or three million innocent noncombatants: the children, the women, and the old people. It has saturated the unfertile soil of Korea by innocent blood, filled millions of souls with bottomless sorrow and millions of bodies with excruciating pain. All this is but a pleasant pastime for the Killer. He calls it mere police action, unworthy even of the term of war.

The Crusader is mighty proud of his deeds. The greater the destruction, the greater his self-admiration. The higher the mountain of corpses, the more generous his self-reward. Lavishly he showers upon his henchmen high ranks and titles, medals and citations, fortune and power, fame and popularity, kisses and copulations.

In the twentieth century, the Destroyer's henchmen have been promoted to the enviable positions of monarchs, presidents, and absolute dictators in the empires; of the high prelates and dignitaries in the religious bodies; of the powerful leaders of labor and agriculture; of the presidents of the greatest universities and foundations; of the potentates of the richest business corporations; of the dictators of the press, radio, television, and movies; of the decisive molders of public opinion; even of the most influential moral authorities. The Killer has successfully convinced the bulk of humanity that his victorious generals and admirals, revolutionary slaughterers and counter-revolutionary executioners are the best candidates for any position, including religious, moral, and educational leadership. Their ability to organize mass murders has been sold as an evidence of ability to discharge any function whatsoever. In our times the Destroyer's big agents are glorified as the greatest heroes. They are extolled as the encyclopedic geniuses of the first magnitude. They fill almost all the top positions in the human universe.

Quite logically the Killer suppresses all the peacemakers and especially the creative peacebuilders. He ridicules them as lunatics and discredits them as morons. If this is not enough, the Destroyer persecutes them as subversives, imprisons them as spies, and executes them as treasonable maniacs. There is no place for peaceful men and women in the kingdom of the Killer. They silently vanish, leaving neither martyr's halo nor any memory.

Now and then in the past the Killer paraded as the Savior of his victims. At the present he invariably masquerades as their hero, their liberator, or their "beloved leader." Not only their life he demands from the doomed, but also their love, and their gratitude for sending them to death, for "saving their soul," or for liberating them from the troubles of living. As Savior he appears in the role of the head of the state sending armies to kill and be killed; in the mask of a victorious general erasing cities from the face of the earth; in the form of a revolutionary leader massacring "the enemies of the people"; in the role of a religious fanatic crusading for the holy war against the heretics; in the image of a humanitarian ideologist preaching "salvation of civilization" through extermination of the barbarians. He is an objective scientist inventing the most efficient means of man's extermination, a labor leader or captain of industry clamoring for prosperity through extermination of the competitors; he is the boss of the press, radio, and other means of communication disseminating hate and strife in the human universe; he is a columnist calling for preventive and repressive wars. There is no end to the variety of the Savior-masks used by the Killer.

His most favored masks in recent times have been three: the grand role of the *liberator* of all the oppressed from all the aggressors; the magnificent mask of the *civilizer* of all the primitive, barbarian, and backward peoples; the noblest role of the *protector* of "our grand civilization, our cultural heritage, and of our magnificent way of life."

As a *liberator* he successfully frees the proletarians from their bourgeois freedom and turns them into full-fledged slaves of his totalitarian state. No less successfully he liberates the peasants and farmers from their land and farms and makes them the "free serfs" of his state henchmen. Most efficiently he unburdens all the preliterate and backward peoples from the yoke of oil, gold, silver, iron, uranium, and diamonds in their land, from harvests in their fields, from precious animals, game, and trees in their forests, from fish, whales, and pearls in their waters. Still more generously he replaces their "wild self-will" by the "civilized freedom" of the dwellers of the social sewers of our megalopolitan cities; by the chained liberty of the pauperized savages in our reservations attended by cultural anthropologists; and by the freedom of "the happy employees" of the benevolent captains of industry and finance. Finally he unselfishly frees any people from an aggressor, possible and impossible. This is his favorite kind of liberation. His technique is truly marvelous: perfectly scientific, economical, simple, and never failing. The liberation consists in a wholesale murder of the victims of the aggressor and in an utter ruin of their country. Korea is a splendid specimen of this sort of liberation. Liberating from life, the Killer frees his beneficiaries from all aggressions and worries. His axiom is: Only the dead are absolutely free.

At present, these Freedom Crusades are going on *fortissimo*. Thousands and thousands are daily graduated into the unlimited freedom of death. Long live the Killing Liberator!

No less remarkable is the Killer's role of the *civilizer*. Those savages who survive his liberations are lovingly subjected to the process of "acculturation." Its first phase consists in a thor-

ough destruction of the total way of life, mores, institutions, and
means of subsistence of the uncivilized peoples. Its second phase
is their complete bewilderment and demoralization. Many savages cannot stand these operations and die; depopulation sets
forth among the accultured patients. For those who survive, a
third phase comes in: they are inculcated with civilized chewing
gum, textiles, alcohol and drugs, a few cheap gadgets, and
venereal diseases. Their songs are replaced by moronish crooning; their beautiful music by urbanized jazz; their beliefs by
a horrible mess of everything from Christ to Lenin. Their
native ethics are supplanted by the inhuman ethics of the civilized slave-masters. The natives are turned into imitative monkeys,
rootless, hungry, despised, exploited, and greedy. Their women
are seduced and ravished. Their property is taken by the civiliz-
ers through "the due process of law." The healthy savages become human derelicts. Lost is their native Garden of Eden.
Human wretches, they move from the social purgatory into the
social sewers of civilization, with its unbearable standard of
living and way of life. Only a few of the savages survive this
civilizational operation. The majority cannot stand it and die.

Thus the great Destroyer proves another axiom of his: *Only
death is the immortal, absolute, and unchangeable form of acculturation.* All other forms of civilization are temporary, relative, and unworthy of a great Civilizer.

Still more impressive is the Destroyer's acting in the role of
the *protector* of "our magnificent civilization, our resplendent
cultural heritage, and of our unmatched way of life." The
actual civilization of the Killer's henchmen is beggarish and their
way of life is rotten. None of them contributes — and can contribute — anything creative to the great cultural values. If anything, they try to destroy these values and to suppress the
creative genius. In spite of this, the henchmen loudly profess
their devotion to great civilization. The role of its protectors

excellently covers their deadly work. It marvelously beautifies
the ugliest deeds they perform under the mask of the defenders
of "our cultural heritage." The resplendent mantle of the
protector of civilization easily screens the most repulsive activities they carry on.

Under this pretext, the henchmen suppress, imprison, and
condemn to death the truly creative geniuses. Any genius creates
something new and different from the existing values. The
Killer's agents never fail to accuse such a deviant of being subversive and dangerous. Their hue and cry is broadcast everywhere and molds public opinion. The result is that the Athenian
Committee on Un-Athenian Activities condemns to death the
most subversive Socrates; the Jewish Committee on Un-Jewish
Activities crucifies Jesus as the greatest criminal; the French-
Catholic Committee on Un-French-Catholic activities burns
Joan of Arc as a heretic; so also does the Geneva Calvinist Committee on Subversive Activities condemn Servetus. In a similar
manner acts the French Revolutionary Committee on Counter-
Revolutionary Subversive Activities in guillotining Lavoisier:
"The Revolution does not need scientists." The Russian revolution re-enacts this drama on a gigantic scale and executes several
million counter-revolutionary subversives.

This operation of the Destroyer has been carried on indefatigably throughout the whole of human history. The "protectors of civilization" have suppressed and killed as many
creative nonconformists as they could grab. Condemned as the
most dangerous subversives, some 37 per cent of the Christian
saints died the death of martyrs. Hundreds and thousands of
the creative minds perished as heretics in the fire and dungeons
of the Inquisition — "the Protection of the Catholic Civilization."
Hundreds and thousands suffered from the Protestant Committees on Un-Protestant Activities, as atheists, as heretics, as
witches, and as Catholics. Some 80 per cent of the greatest

philosophers, social scientists, and moral teachers have been either imprisoned or banished or condemned to death or tortured or had to flee to save their lives, or have been penalized in other ways by various "protectors of civilization and culture." In a lesser degree the same is true of the great creators in the fine arts, in politics and economics.

At the present time, the great Destroyer plays this role on a grand scale. In each country there are his Committees on Un-Committees Subversive Activities, exterminating all the suspicious nonconformists. In the Communist countries they massacre all the non-Communist subversives; in the anti-Communist countries, they suppress all "the Communist rats" and their Fellow Travelers. As time goes on, the work of these "Committees on the Mutual Extermination of Human Beings" becomes increasingly exciting, hotter, and more efficient in its murderous power. It rapidly progresses from the daily quota of a few victims to those of hundreds, thousands, and tens of thousands. Respectively its name changes from "suppression of a few subversives" to "cold war" and "police action" and finally to "world war."

At the present these operations of the Killer's direct executioners are enormously helped by the honey-tongued professors and columnists, by the silky-mouthed preachers and artists, by the "very, very idealistic" ideologists in the anti-Communist countries, and by the "very, very materialistic" ideologists in the Communist nations. These parasites of the bloodsucking parasite-executioners are manufacturing tons of ideologies of the "Protection of Our Civilization" and "Our Cultural Heritage." In the name of these they clamor for a pitiless extermination of all the opponents; for a total destruction of the alien ways of life; and for a suppression of all the non-conformist ideologists. Their highly perfumed words successfully hide the hideous smell of the rotten bodies of their victims. When exposed, their high-

falutin moral is familiar: "If I steal my neighbor's wife, it is good
and protects our civilization; if somebody else steals my wife,
it is bad and it destroys our cultural heritage." They well see
the speck in the eye of their neighbors and they are blind to
the timber in their own eye. Wonderful Protectors of civilization!

This whole operation demonstrates once more the superhuman skill of the Great Destroyer. He fully succeeds in
achieving his horrible task through the most beautiful-looking
and most nobly dressed operations.

The Great Destroyer has always been cunning and mighty.
In our times he is omniscient and omnipotent. He is super-
scientific in the organization of the machinery of destruction.
He is superhumanly powerful in turning everything into ashes.
He is the greatest genius in confusing minds, in deadening con-
science, and in dulling the sense of beauty. His propaganda of
falsehoods is more effective than the gospel of the Word of
God.

In a few weeks, out of millions of good youth he organizes
armies of terrific killers. In a few hours he atomizes millions
of human beings into smoky nothingness. In a few minutes he
leaves an abomination of desolation of what was before a
metropolis or prosperous country. In a few days he utterly
uglifies the beautiful face of the earth.

He does all this cold-bloodedly, scientifically, and methodically.
There is nothing on this planet that can oppose his destructive
might. He has all the power of a nihilistic science, all the
strength of the morally indifferent technology, and all the
might of boundless hatred.

Still more magnificent is the efficiency of his propaganda.
He can manipulate public opinion as he pleases. Through his
blaring radios and televisions, screaming headlines and movies;
through his "ennobling" plays and "inspiring" civic parades;

through his "purifying" religious ceremonies and "enlightening" forums; through his "educational" sports and "edifying" lectures; through his gigantic machinery of thought control, he successfully convinces 95 per cent of mankind that black is white, good is bad, virtue is evil, ugliness is beauty, and madness is wisdom.

And especially striking is the success of his ethics of murder. He strongly disapproves killing of only one or a few individuals. He calls such actions "felonious crimes" and mercilessly punishes their criminal perpetrators.

In contrast to that, the Great Perverter is most enthusiastic about the killing of thousands and millions. He calls these mass slaughters by the reverent names of "patriotic wars," "heroic revolutions," "noblest crusades of liberation," or "sacred evangelizing" — all honorable and saintly, all blessed by God, sanctified by ethics, justified by law, and glorified by the arts and sciences.

He brilliantly proves that exactly this mass murder was what Jesus hallowed in his Sermon on the Mount; what was blessed by Jehovah in the Ten Commandments, was consecrated by Buddha in his Dhammapada, made holy by the Bhagavad Gita, extolled by Lao-Tse and Confucius, preached by Zoroaster and Mahavira, taught by Plato and Aristotle, and approved by all-religious and atheistic-moral teachers of humanity. Through thousands of his mouthpieces — theologians and philosophers, scientists and politicians, artists and educators, journalists and preachers, generals and admirals — the Great Perverter easily persuades humanity of "these self-evident truths." Exactly for this reason each operation of mass murder is preceded and followed either by invocation of God's blessing of, or by atheistic consecration of, the bigger and bloodier murders; it is hallowed by the presence of priests or political commissars among the fighters for fanning the bloodshed spark into a gigantic conflagration *ad majorem gloriam Dei*, Fatherland, or Communistic paradise. For this reason, "Thou shalt not kill" is now branded as a subversive insanity; "Love thine enemies" is prosecuted as treason; and the conscientious objectors are imprisoned and executed.

Finally, the Unholy seals the truth of his faith by the impressive commemoration of his biggest slaughters and of their eminent leaders. He immortalizes them in thousands of monuments, buildings, sculptures, pictures, coins, medals, poems, plays, symphonies, festivals, holy days, parades, games, commemorative prizes and distinctions. The gigantic bloodsheds are turned into the landmarks of epochs and eras; their leaders, into glorified supermen and gods. The propaganda machinery of the Killer is indeed irresistible.

As to the small minority of recalcitrants, the Destroyer disposes of them easily and simply. Prison, torture, gallows, shooting squad, guillotine, electric chair, and gas chamber efficiently exterminate the insensate nonconformists and their followers. Often a mere threat of these "educational correctives" is enough to convert the heretics quickly into believers of the Great Perverter.

. . . The Perverter is the thousand-faced Janus. His masks are illimitable in diversity. His personality is endlessly changing. So also are his aliases, occupations, addresses, and social stations. Now he appears in one, now in another form. In a small dose he is *in every one of us*. Each of us daily contributes directly or indirectly to his harvest. Once in a while, in the moments of our madness, we become the Perverter's tools; fortunately, not too often and not entirely.

More frequently he incarnates himself *in the ruling groups; in the governments of the empires and powers — political and economic; and in their advisers — scientific and legal.* For this reason the *ruling groups have always had the highest rate of the most brutal, greedy, selfish, sensual, and cynical individuals.*

Compared with other social groups, the governments, statesmen, and politicians have ordinarily had the highest percentage of the worst murderers: *patricides, matricides, fratricides, uxoricides, filicides, up to the predatory killers of one's own intimate friends and benefactors.* For the same reason, the ruling groups have harbored the highest quota of lesser criminals: cheaters, forgers, thieves, robbers, brigands, seducers, rapists, polygamists, sexual perverts, and other varieties of *homo criminalis.* There are few, if any, ordinary criminals who can compete in all these crimes with especially the tops of the ruling groups, like Sulla and Marius, Caesar and Augustus, Galerius and Constantine the Great, William the Conqueror and Henry the Eighth, John the Terrible and Peter the Great, Catherine the Great and Elizabeth the Great, Louis the Fourteenth and Napoleon, the Ten and the Thirty Tyrants, Cromwell and Robespierre, Lenin and Stalin, Hitler and Mussolini, Genghis Khan and Tamerlane, Attila and Suleiman, the Borgias and Pizarro and other "greats" of the political and business empires. While among the common mortals there are a few human tools of the Unholy among the ruling groups he finds them many times more and fills them with an incomparably deadlier hatred and destructive insanity.

Though the ruling groups make an insignificant fraction of the human population, they have exterminated, directly and indirectly, more human beings than one half of the ruled. The favorite symbolic nicknames and emblems of members of the governing class points at the same carnivorous propensity: "the Lion," "the Tiger," "the Eagle," "the Falcon," "the Hawk," "the Snake," "the Cobra," "the Terrible," "the Serpent," the "Scourge of God," "the Iron," "the Conqueror," "the Invincible," "the Destroyer," "the Fearsome," "the Whip of Destiny," "the Pitiless," "the Unmerciful," "the Remorseless," "the Hammer," and so on. In a diluted form these homicidal tendencies are quite frequent among the minor members of the ruling groups, from the corrupt ward politician and crooked judge up to the higher political bullies, heartless inquisitors and executioners.

. . . All-compassionate Soul of the World! Save us, the little human creatures, from the imminent perdition of our souls and the death of our bodies. We are helpless to save ourselves. There is no one else whom we can ask for help. Even our Mighty Leaders are against us. Even our Exalted Rulers are deaf to our lamentations. Only Thine command can change them out of the vainglorious agents of the Destroyer into the humble servants of Thine Kingdom, and Love, and Pity!

S.O.S.

CHAPTER TWO

Supplications of the Little Mortals
to the Big Immortals

Your Superhuman Majesties! and Your Incomparable Highnesses!

Your Divine Holinesses and Your Heavenly Eminencies!

Majestic Presidents! Omnipotent Dictators!

Imperturbable Demiurges of the United Nations!

Magnificent Marshalissimos, Generalissimos, and Admiralissimos!

Incorruptible Dispensers of Justice!

Superpotent Rulers of Business Empires!

Impeccable Emperors of Labor Unions!

Resplendent Diplomats, Wisest Senators, and Artful Politicians!

Omniscient Scientists and Infallible Experts!

Sovereign Sultans of Communist, Socialist, Fascist, Republican, Democratic, Monarchical, Left, Right, and Center Political Leviathans!

And Ye, Saintly Educators of Our Soul, University Presidents and Deans, Professors and Doctors!

And Ye, Irresistible Deities of Screen, Stage, Radio, and Television!

And Ye, Incorruptible Publishers and Editors. And Ye, Virginally Pure Columnists and Commentators!

And Ye, Molders and Pollers of Public Opinion!

And Ye, Stars of the Human Universe who blind our mortal eyes by Your Brilliancy!

And All Ye, who hold us mortals in the hollow of Your hand and control our destiny by the tip of Your finger!

Bend Your glorious ear to our pious supplications. Do not turn Your immortal face from the little worms we are. For we, the miserable wretches, are sinking in the bottomless pit of grief, hatred, and death. Listen graciously to our lamentations. Do not wrathfully condemn us for ever and ever to the inferno we are writhing in. Deliver us by Your power and wisdom from the serpent of strife that is swallowing us. Bring us by Your limitless glory into the light of peaceful life. For Yours is the Grace and the Potency to save our Freudian souls from Oedipus' incest, sadism and masochism, from patricide, matricide, and the total extermination of everyone by everyone.

Ye, All-glorious Immortals! Your providential ways are inscrutable to us. Our chicken brain cannot understand the infinite mind of Yours. Neither do we dare to question Your incomprehensible wisdom. By Your gracious leave, we can only pray for Your merciful enlightenment. We, Your humblest servants, earnestly implore Ye, brilliant Stars of the Human Universe, to enlighten us, how and why have we come to our *dies irae, dies illa?* For what reason has Your illimitable kindness engineered the expiatory sacrifice of many millions of us, the mortal sinners, in the First World War, then in the Russian and other revolutions, then in the Second World War and in endless wars and police actions, in revolts and counter-revolutions that have followed these gigantic sacrifices? Wherefore has Your boundless love decreed the destruction of one fifth of the inhabited area of this planet, of our cities and villages, homes and churches, schools and factories, hospitals and museums, fields and orchards? For what reason, Ye, All-mercifuls and All-compassionates have condemned to die and to rot more than one hundred millions of young, vigorous, and beautiful bodies that have not lived yet even one third of the normal span of human life? Why has Your superhuman justice ordered the bottomless agony and mental torture, unbearable pain and unglorious death not only for the grown-up sinners among us but also for our helpless and innocent children who have not had time as yet to sin and to commit any violation of Your commandments? If we, the old sinners, must be punished, why are these innocents subjected to the infernal ordeal? Why have Ye, our Lords and Protectors, unleashed the infinite fury of merciless hate, instead of the all-ennobling love, in our human universe?

Is it because "whom the Lord loveth, he chasteneth; and scourgeth every son whom He receiveth"? If so, have Your mercy upon us! We are scourged beyond our endurance. Your indefatigable chastisements send us quickly into the grave. Your "love" brings our premature death. We cannot comprehend such a love. It passeth our understanding. It looks to us more similar to hate than to love, as we know these experiences.

Is it because Your wisdom wanted to re-enact the greatest mystery of all mysteries, the eternal *Agnus Dei qui tollis peccata mundi?* Alas! We are not the lambs of God. We cannot redeem even our own sins, not to mention the sins of the world. Only Ye, the unclimbable Majesties and unscaleable Highnesses, can perform this miracle. And yet, Ye have not done it. Instead, ever-increasing millions of us, insignificant gnats, are being sacrificed year by year. Why and wherefore we know not. Since Your immortal face, undismayed, continues to radiate joy at our sufferings, since Ye assure us that we are not perishing in vain, Ye must certainly have sufficient reasons for all this slaughtering and destruction.

Pray, enlighten us in our ignorance. Forgive us our crooked ways in order that we can pass our numbered days in peace and contentment. Allow us to earn honestly our daily bread; to rear our children for life, and not for death; to participate in the creation of imperishable values; to lift ourselves, once in a while, into the realm of the eternal light, and to enjoy now and then, side by side with life's sorrows, the pure joys of living. And, finally, our numbered days running out, permit us to die peacefully without murdering anyone or being murdered. We are mortally tired from our ordeal and want peace in our souls and peace on this beautiful suffering earth. Pray, enlighten us and help us, Ye Inscrutable Immortals!

REMONSTRATIONS OF THE BLASPHEMERS AGAINST THE IMPERTURBABLE POWERS

Our Lordly Guardians! The worst catastrophe happened. A new unredeemable Fall occurred. The most impatient among us could not stand Your endless scourging any more. Inspired by Satan himself, they revolted. They began to ask impertinent questions, to address blasphemous petitions, to doubt Your infallible wisdom, and to utter unforgivable curses against Your protective guidance. By this sacrilege they sealed not only their own doom, but endangered also the souls of other mortals.

With the Devil's help, their insanity proves now to be contagious. Their dreadful example is now being imitated by ever-increasing thousands of the chastised humans. They also begin to question disrespectfully, to petition impudently, and, *horribile dictu!* to curse You sacrilegiously.

We, the faithful, are deeply dismayed by this catastrophe. For our own sake and for the sake of others we want to stop the mad epidemics. We humbly solicit Your help in this task. We reverently beseech Ye, the Shining Suns of the Human Universe, to reveal to us the crushing answers to the questions of our hell-bound blasphemers. They torment our souls with these questions and find our answers unconvincing. Bless us

with Your revelations unassailable by any revolter and unquestionably persuading everyone by their truth "or else." . . .

We reverently bring to Ye, our Lords, these blasphemous
questions in an expurgated, softened, and purified form. Re-
ceive them magnanimously and bless us with Your revelations.

DEVOUT PROTESTATIONS AGAINST THE EXECUTIONERS OF HISTORY

On the wings of the fragrant smoke of burning cities and
villages our prayer rises first of all to You, Omnipotent Lenins,
Stalins, Hitlers, Titos, Mussolinis, and all the Bloodiest Dictators
of all the most frenzied civil strifes, revolutionary and reactionary.

Like Your numberless predecessors Ye did not hesitate to set
fire to the house of millions of human dwellers and to call for
an unlimited extermination of all the enemies of the people, of
all the exploiters of laboring classes, of all the rich and aristo-
cratic, of all the masters of serfs and the lords of slaves, of all
the upper castes, orders, and classes; and of everyone who in some
way stood in the way of Your providential dictatorship. Without
any vacillation, You ordered to be destroyed anything and
everything that opposed Your endeavors.

In all these efforts You have been motivated, of course, only
by the highest and purest motives — to liberate all the oppressed,
to equalize opportunities for all, to provide freedom and justice,
mental, moral, and social progress of the whole humanity, to
exterminate disease, insanity, crime, poverty, suffering, stupidity,
and unhappiness in mankind; to establish a New Heaven on this
unhappy planet. Nothing selfish, nothing corrupt, nothing
debased has motivated Your divine mission.

You justly pride Yourselves on Your magnificent success in
the extermination of all Your enemies and in a planetary destruction. In the Russian revolution alone at least twenty-five

millions of the "enemies of the people" have been sacrificed to Your God of the Revolution. The enormous Eurasian country was utterly destroyed during the first few years of the Communist bloody baptism. Still larger are the contributions to Death and Destruction of the Chinese revolution. Smaller on an absolute scale, but no stingier in proportion to the size of the nation, are the votive offerings of human flesh and the destructive offertories to the Gods of Civil Strife by Ye, the invincible Francos, Ye, seventy-seven star generals and Titos, and by Ye, the other smaller deities of reaction and double-crossing. Taken together in this century alone, Ye, the Dictatorial Saviors of Humanity, generously sacrificed uncounted millions of us, the expendable human beings, and destroyed more material and immaterial values than all the tornadoes, hurricanes, floods, earthquakes, and epidemics taken together. Your potency exceeds the wild forces of nature! Your Titanic Imperturbability transcends even the quiet poise of a boa constrictor swallowing its victim.

Even our Inferno-doomed revolters admit these Titanic achievements of Your Revolutionary Majesties and Your Counter-Revolutionary Grandiosities. Their blasphemy begins with their impudent claim that all these sacrifices, destructions, and sufferings have been in vain; that in spite of the tremendous price You paid, at the cost of the others, to Your Idols of Revolution and the Molochs of Counter-Revolution, Your Gods and Ye, their Prophets, have not delivered the goods You promised. The blasphemers madly contend that nothing good for mankind or for the oppressed, the poor, the low, and the proletarian classes has come out of Your merciless murder and frenzied destruction. Neither freedom, nor creativity, nor mental, moral, aesthetic, vital, and material improvement has resulted from Your masochistic and sadistic mania. The unrepentant sinners question even the purity of Your motives.

They insist that Ye, Our Himalayan Giants, are most selfish and brutal, most power-drunk and greedy, most sensual and beastly, much worse than the worst of the ordinary criminals. The heretics deride even Your mental capacity. They call Ye, the Titans, stupid, idiotic, devoid of any constructive creativity and endowed only with extraordinary brutality and cynical cunning.

The doomed sinners say that Ye cannot tolerate any creative genius and either kill him or suppress his creativity. They point out further that in spite of all Your horrible offertories to the Killer and Destroyer, today's material standard of the masses is lower than it was before the Chinese revolution of 1911 . . . the Russian revolution of 1917 . . . and the Fascist, the Nazi, the Franco, the Tito, and the other revolutions of our age. The sacrilegious grumblers indignantly demonstrate the catastrophic decline of freedom of all kinds and the enormous growth of Your totalitarian tyranny and regimentation. They claim further that through Your upstart efforts, misery, disease, insanity, criminality, and ignorance in the human universe have greatly increased while the true creativity has notably decreased.

These miseducated wretches say, moreover, that none of the violent revolutions and counter-revolutions have ever benefited anyone except Ye, the Executioners of History, and Your immediate henchmen. If some benefit has occurred, for somebody else, it has been a thousand times overbalanced by the disastrous consequences of the inhuman violence. The mislearned seditionaries firmly point out that all the bloody disturbances beginning with the earliest recorded communist revolution in Ancient Egypt, c. 3000 B.C., and passing through all the bloody Babylonian, Hindu, Chinese, Iranian, Greek, Roman, and Euro-American revolutions up to the most recent ones, have destroyed incomparably more than created, killed more than revived, brutalized more than ennobled. Besides their own proofs, the perverted heretics refer to the greatest thinkers of all times as stating the same verities. Ipuver and Neferrohe, Lao-Tse and Con-

fucius, Buddha and Mahavira, Jesus and Zoroaster, Plato and
Aristotle, Herodotus and Thucydides, St. Paul and St. Augustine,
St. Thomas Aquinas and Luther, up to J. de Maistre and Cha-
teaubriand, Tolstoy and Dostoevski, H. Taine and other recent observers of the violent internal disturbances: they all
assert the deadly and unholy results of unlimited violence. They
all impiously call Ye, the Liberators of the Oppressed, by the
names of "Bloody Upstarts," "Unholy Tyrants," "Worst of
the Beasts," "Executioners of History," and other blasphemous
titles. They deride Your revolution and counter-revolutions as
crocodiles that devour first the fat and the rich, then the poor
and the emaciated, and finally, the revolutionaries and their
leaders themselves. Thus they revile Your Gods, Yourselves,
and Your followers.

Their impious ignorance is so great that they do not distinguish
much between the Revolutionary Majesties and the Counter-
Revolutionary Grandiosities among Ye, our Lords. "They are
two shoes of the same pair," they assert, and which shoe is
worse it is hard to decide. Both are bad. Both gangs are made up
of brutes believing in and practicing unrestrained violence.

To both of Your Great Parties these blasphemers oppose themselves as the worshipers of non-violence and non-violent resistance to evil. This subversive sect is too cowardly to fight
valiantly and take an eye for an eye and a tooth for a tooth
with a big dividend. Instead, they profess a despicable meekness and practice the treasonable "love thine enemy" and "blessed
are the merciful, the peacemakers, the pure in heart," and similar bosh. Luckily, the number of these seditious lunatics is
small and they are not dangerous. Rejecting the wisdom of this
world and aspiring for the fantastic foolishness with God, they
simply do not have any power to carry out anything. Their
non-violent resistance cannot resist even a small detachment of
police. At any moment they can be destroyed by a company of
green soldiers. They are regularly imprisoned, banished, and

executed by Your secret and open henchmen in all Your revolutions and counter-revolutions. Only in the existing exceptional conditions do they become a real danger.

Ye, All-mighty Earth-Shakers, can easily remove this menace. If You reveal to us Your crushing answers to the remonstrations of the seditionaries, and add a few of Your scourings and Your liberations through death, the revolters will vanish, leaving no trace of their existence. With their liquidation, our bodies shall remain unbroken and our souls shall be redeemed. Glory to Ye, Invincible Conquerors of all the enemies of the people, Mighty Overthrowers of all obsolescent regimes, Destroyers of the non-violent devotees of the "foolishness with God" and "love thine enemy." Let Your Power blossom forever and ever!

Humblest Admonitions to the Legitimate Executives of History

Your Paramount Superiorities, the Kings of Kings, the Presidents of Presidents, the Super-Secretaries and Supra Cabinet Ministers, the Supertowering Senators and the High-Mountainous Representatives! Ever-Poised Diplomats and Never-Disturbed Ambassadors! And Ye, the United Nations' Designers of Peace, Combiners of Police Actions, and Creators of the "Never Cease Fire" Miracles!

If Ye heard our complimentary remonstrations to the Illegitimate Upstarts of Revolutions and Counter-Revolutions, we beseech Ye to forgive us for this flattery. Since our numbered days are a mere handbreadth to the Upstart Majesties, and since our flesh is as the grass that withereth at the slightest deviation from "the general line" in the Dictatorships, we can prolong the fleeting life of our bodies here only by flattering the Upstarts and by inflating their lilliputian balloons to the magnitude of the largest galaxies of the universe.

Our loyalty and patriotic fervor belong only to Ye, the Lawful, the Legitimate, and the Incorruptible Rulers duly insured by the Grace of God or by the officially certified will of the people or by the inviolate inheritance of all the exalted ranks and positions of Your titled fathers and crowned forefathers. Ye are our shield and in Ye we put our trust. Tax us, draft us, send us to kill or be killed, use us as Ye please. We, the loyal expendables, shall not be found grumbling. And if, in Your magnanimity, now and then Ye pin a medal on our breast, or publicly pronounce a citation in our honor, or promote us to a higher rung of the heaven-bound ladder of precedences, we shall not be wanting. Even our dead brothers shall be rejoicing at the badges Ye posthumously grant to their rotting bodies.

Omnipotent Rulers of the Human Universe! We deplore to report to You that a portion of our former brothers defected the flock of Your faithful and fell into the clutches of the Tempter. They joined the madhouse of the lunatics of meekness and non-violence, peace and unselfish love. After joining it, they behave now as seditiously as all these lunatics do in regard to all the Legitimate Authorities and Illegitimate Powers on this planet. Until their poisonous tongues are extirpated, their foolish mouths utter endless blasphemies against You — You whom no blasphemy can touch and no verbal, non-violent attack can disturb at all. The impious insulters seemingly do not know that Your spiritual skin is bulletproof, and remorseless, shielded against any regret and sense of guilt, insulated against any compassion and morbid self-criticism. We, Your faithful slaves, now humbly report to You the digest of the blasphemies of the lunatics of mercy, forgiveness, and non-violence.

The blasphemers say that Ye, the lawful Executives of History, do not differ much from the Upstart Rulers. Some of Ye are even worse than the Upstart Executioners of History. In the lunatics' opinion, these have at least some vigor in tearing down rotten

social edifices while many of You are but the impotent and degenerated posterity of Your great forefathers. You have all the
vices of Your eminent ancestors but none of their virtues; neither
brains, nor creativity, nor licentious courage, nor unselfish devotion to the tribe, nor even reckless and open amorality. The
Upstarts are openly cynical, materialistic and atheistic; they
shamelessly boast their vices while You are hypocrites, full of
secret depravities and cancerous perversions. The Upstarts
blindly destroy but now and then build something. The senile
among You just drift and let drift. Impotent to create, they cannot even tear down the crumbling institutions. They simply
rot and let rot.

In other words, in the perverted opinion of the crazy "peacemakers," You, the Legitimate Executives of History, are about
as bad as the Illegitimate Executioners of History. In our age
both of You serve mainly the Great Killer and the unholy
Perverter instead of serving the Oversoul and the humble, the
needy, and the suffering.

Your training and the machinery that selects and appoints
You to Your exalted positions make out of You about as un-
Godly a group as the group of Upstarts. Both groups contain
a higher rate of arch-murderers — patricides, matricides, fratricides, uxoricides, filicides, and so on — than any other social
stratum, not to mention the ordinary killers, robbers, brigands,
burglars, thieves, perjurers, forgers, traitors, rapists, adulterers,
kidnapers, torturers, and the variety of other felonous and lesser
criminals among You. Except for the population of the peni-
tentiaries, there is no other social group so highly criminal as
You, the Executives and the Executioners of History.

In lying and perfidy, however, You excel all the other groups,
even the professional criminals. You elevate these vices into
the artistic Cult of Diplomacy with its ritualistic protocol and
ceremonious pomp and etiquette. The most predatory and most

shameless liars are glorified by Ye as the "great diplomats," "the famous Secretaries of State," "the eminent Ministers of Foreign Affairs," "the Resplendent Plenipotentiaries."

In Your Hall of Fame and in Your histories the greatest diplomatic liars, forgers, and perjurers are given as much glory and space as the most merciless killers and destroyers among Your statesmen. The more shameless the deceit and the larger the massacre, the greater the glorification of Your monarchs and presidents, prime ministers and dictators, generals and admirals, diplomats and bureaucrats. Your lust for this sort of infamous glory is unquenchable. You earnestly believe that every creature and human being, and even all the suns and moons of heaven, are created only for Your use and for singing the glorious dithyrambs to Your diplomatic and military exploits.

The seditious lunatics charge further that at the present time You serve mainly the Great Killer and Destroyer and hardly render any service to God and humanity. The lunatics back their accusations by pointing at the two world wars, by the preparations for the Third World War, by the innumerable smaller wars, revolutions, and counter-revolutions of this century, started, engineered, and carried out by You, the Policemen and Gangsters of History. The ever-increasing millions of corpses, the ever-expanding blood-saturated area on this planet, the progressively growing ruins of what was the great civilization of humanity — all this is directly charged to You by the blasphemers. They call You the *Ghouls and Vultures of History* that fatten on human corpses and on ruins. Your life, Your fortune, Your fame, Your happiness, Your titles and medals, honors and exalted ranks — all are made and earned through Your service to the Great Killer and Destroyer.

If there were no wars, no revolutions, and no devastations, none of You would have had anything from Your fame, titles, fortune, and power. In a peaceful society there is no need for

war-making monarchs, generals, admirals, revolutionary executioners, diplomatic liars, and other varieties of the wreckers
of civilization and organizers of mass murder. In a peaceful
human universe You would be nothing but the *Unemployed
of History*, living by charity and by odd jobs. Where there
are no corpses and blood, no graves and smoking ruins, there
are no ghouls and vultures, no executioners — and no victims.
Incessant mass murder and destruction is the absolute necessity
of Your "to be or not to be." Without these there is no place
for You in human history.

Our Glorious Lords! The poisonous tongues of the blasphemers do not stop at these profanities. They accuse You of
many other evils. They say that in our age You are the wreckers
of prosperity and freedom, of the family and good morality, of
creativity and happiness, of vitality and the survival of nations.
You wreck economic prosperity and natural resources directly,
through Your devastating wars and destructions. In a few days
Your armies destroy what has been created by the labor of millions for generations. In a few hours You turn into a poisonous
smoke the gigantic cities and blossoming fields with all their
inestimable values — material and spiritual, cultural and natural. In a few moments You annihilate what demanded the creative efforts of the greatest geniuses and countless numbers of
craftsmen and laborers.

As a finishing irony, after the destruction of the cities and
inhabited areas, You benevolently appoint Committees for the
Restoration, Preservation, and Development of Civilization. The
scholarly members of these committees begin carefully to
catalogue and put into museums a few surviving derelicts of
painting and sculpture, architecture and music, theaters and
churches, museums and libraries, gadgets and factories of the
destroyed cities and countries. By Your order they set aside
a Token Fund for "the point seven" of Your restoration and

development program. In comparison with the funds for Your rearmament and war program, this Restoration Fund is so insignificant that it cannot buy even the coffins for the victims of Your wars and rearmaments.

Having ruined whole continents, You and Your committees generously build a few hospitals and a dozen feeding points insufficient to take care of even Your own myrmidons wounded in the struggle. Your hypocrisy is so great, however, that You shamelessly boast of Your generosity and humanity and eventually Yourselves begin to believe these delusions. By these gestures You cover Your unholy deeds by the mantle of High Protectors of Culture. And the "cultured" members of Your committees never fail to compose eloquent hymns to Your role of the Saviors of Civilization. Here, as elsewhere, the scholarly members of governmentally appointed Committees turn out to be but the parasites of the destroyers of humanity.

Besides the direct ruining of prosperity, You wreck it indirectly by Your exorbitant taxes — in money and blood — for the maintenance of Your armies, Your legions of bureaucrats, Your henchmen. These leeches suck the greater part of the economic juice from Your subjects and serfs. By Your channeling the wealth-making labor and resources into the armament industries, You impoverish humanity still more: nobody can eat Your atom bombs or Your guns, or enjoy Your poisonous gas and deadly bacterias. If mankind had not had You and Your ways of insane waste and prodigious destruction of economic values, humanity's standard of living would have been now at least as high as Your own conspicuous consumption. In fact, You and Your destructive activities have been and are now the main factor of human poverty and economic misery.

Our Protectors and Defenders! The seditious fanatics call You Tyrants, Muzzlers, and Suffocators of Freedom. It is Your nature, they say, to regiment compulsorily and to control coercively, under penalties of this or that sort, everyone and everything You can command. Until there is a resistance to Your unlimited lust for domination, You cannot help expanding Your tyrannical regimentation. If we, the mortals, were not resisting indefatigably this lust of Yours, nothing would have been left of our freedom and rights. We mortals would have been turned long ago into mechanical puppets pulled and pushed by Your strings.

At the present time, Your lust for unlimited Totalitarian Despotism is especially strong. In the countries of the Upstart Rulers it has reached its maximum potential. The Executioners of History there regiment the whole life of their subjects from the cradle to the grave. The population is turned into a real puppetry entirely controlled by the Rulers. The only freedom left to human beings is the assurance of the Upstarts that puppets are perfectly free to follow the Executioners' commands or else to die before firing squads, in prisons, or in labor camps. Through their secret police and open henchmen, through fully monopolized press, radio, television, movies, theaters, and other means of communication, through prohibition of any deviation from the rigid "general line" of the government, the Upstarts control not only the minds and behavior of their subjects but even their physiological functions. In comparison with the Totalitarian Upstarts' tyranny, the despotism of the police states of the Absolute Monarchies is quite liberal and soft. In comparison with Stalin-Hitler's control, the regimentation of the Egyptian pharaohs, of Diocletian and Constantine the Great, of Louis the Fourteenth and Peter the Great, was mild and limited.

In the so-called "democratic countries," the situation is not so bad as in the Upstarts' nations, but it is rapidly moving in the same direction. The totalitarian regimentation of everything, beginning with prices and wages and ending with ideas, beliefs, and tastes, is rapidly growing while the freedom of the citizens

to manage their own affairs, life, and relationships is fast withering. The secret police are increasingly becoming the supreme
judges of one's subversiveness or loyalty. The Parliament or the
Congress is degenerating into the inquisitional Star Chamber,
imprisoning political nonconformists and punishing undesirable
deviationists. The prisons are becoming more and more populated. The nonconformists are muzzled, imprisoned, and discharged from good positions, doomed to starve slowly and to
die. The school, the church, the family, the unions, societies,
associations, and organizations are increasingly taken under the
control of the Rulers. They appoint their henchmen as the presidents, the chiefs, and the directors of all institutions. Already
they regiment and manage a vital part of the national business.
They militarize and governmentalize the whole culture and the
way of life of their countries. They terrorize most of the possible opponents. They vilify the opposition. In brief, the
Legitimate Rulers rapidly become totalitarian and tyrannical
and progressively approach the unlimited *jus vitae ac necis,* the
right of life and death, of the Upstart Tyrants. The political
regimes of all nations are tending to become regimes of big
prisons with the whole population regimented by merciless
totalitarian wardens who are unlimited in their liberty by any
law, who limit the liberty of the inmates to the zero level. A
new slavery is developing before our eyes.

The subversive lunatics accuse You, the Givers of All Boons,
of the *disintegration of the family and the demoralization of the
rank and file.* Through drafting the youth into the armed forces,
You, Our Masters, separate children from their parents. By
drafting husbands you break the marriage bond between man
and wife. By separating the married for a long time You cultivate adultery and disloyalty. Your sending wives and women
to factories and offices undermines the family and marriage.
By plunging green youth into the atmosphere of the murderous

business, You steer their sexual life into the prostitutional channels with their venereal disease, utter vulgarity, and frequent criminality. This again weakens the family and marriage. In dozens of other ways You contribute to this pernicious result. And what is perhaps the worst is Your hypocrisy in this matter. In Your pompous speeches You always parade as the Virginal Knights of the Family, as the Protectors of the Sanctity of Marriage, and as the Faithful Crusaders of Chastity and Virginity. In Your own family life You are hardly better than open prostitutes. Fancifully changing Your wives and husbands, mistresses and lovers, committing all possible sexual crimes and sex perversions, You send the members of Your families to death or prison more frequently than does any other social group. You supply us, the common mortals, with the worst examples of rotten family and faithless marriage. By the objective consequences of Your political measures You undermine the family more than any other group. If Your Research Committees on the Family do not mention Your destructive role, the reason is simple: they are well paid for their peculiar blindness and they know well whence come their butter and bread. In addition, they do not want to be purged and lose their scholarly prestige and benefits. In their silence about these points, they simply imitate Your own hypocrisy of seeing what is not there and not seeing what is there; of saying what is pleasant to the bosses and keeping unspoken what is unpleasant. They simply follow the old rule of the *captatio benevolentiae*.

Ever-Shining Moral Stars and Never-Erring Legal Guides of the ruled mortals! The blasphemous seditionists go completely berserk when they babble of Your moral role. They view You as the *Perverters and Demoralizers* of Your faithful flocks, as the most criminal group among all human groups. The lunatics back this crazy statement by statistics of crimes allegedly showing that the ruling groups generally give the highest quota of murderers and criminals of all kinds. They viciously claim that this is especially true of the ruling classes of our age. In the berserkers' opinion, these classes are rotten from the top to the bottom. They are the main agents of the Great Killer and Destroyer. No wonder, they say, that the existing ruling groups and the criminal gangs are twins, inseparable from each other, with the Rulers being the worse of the pair. No wonder, they continue, that the machineries of the ruling parties and of the criminal gangs are interlocked and overlapping. No surprise that the prevalent personality type of the Rulers and of the criminal leaders is essentially similar.

The seditionists assert that Your moral influence is extremely disastrous. Your personal example radiates the very widest imitation by Your flocks. The corruption of the Immortals stimulates the corruption of the mortals. The cynicism of the Rulers breeds nihilism of the ruled. If the monarchs and presidents, red and black dictators, generals and admirals, secretaries and cabinet ministers, senators and representatives, members of the United Nations and of other bodies politic approve and commit criminal actions on a large scale and get away with it, the common people cannot help but follow their example. If the Great Leaders eloquently preach the glory of "patriotic" mass murder of the innocent millions, including children and women, by atom bombing, by saturated bombing, by any destructive means available, the flock is easily convinced that this Perverter's ethics is what God, Jesus, Buddha, or some other moral teacher commands. If, in addition to preaching, the Rulers practice these Satanic precepts by actual killing of the innocent millions, their demoralizing role turns out to be truly catastrophic. They effectively drag their nations to the very bottom of moral degradation. They succeed in what Satan, tempting Jesus, failed: they sell their unholy deeds as a fulfillment of the commands of the Sermon on the Mount and other true ethical codes. They falsify the very standards of what is good and bad, right and wrong.

The result of this infernal work is the moral degradation of their flocks. Led by the Rulers, the people forget indeed "thou shalt not kill" and replace it by the virtuous Operation Killer. In the name of God they pridefully commit the deeds of Satan. All the restraints and inhibitions of an unlimited murder are forgotten. The last vestiges of elementary decency and international law are thus thrown to the dogs. Instead, "the new ethics of an unlimited murder of an unlimited number of people" — for the sake of survival, victory or mere pleasure — is introduced, rooted, and practiced. Humanity reaches thus the lowest possible moral standard, the standard of the Great Perverter himself. There is no possibility of sinking further.

To ascertain the permanency of this demoralization, the Rulers ingeniously shape the cultural and social institutions of their flocks. They pervade these with the cult of military glory, with the pathos of the my country "right or wrong," by the ethos of patriotic and heroic mass murder, by the spirit of the immortal victory over all the enemies, by the mythology of the fighting forefathers, and so on. They plunge into this atmosphere every newborn baby and keep him there throughout his life. From the child's earliest age, the Rulers teach him to play the role of the fighter, gloriously shooting or cutting the enemies. This role, together with an unconditional obedience to the Rulers — called "patriotic discipline" — is incessantly inculcated into the child in his schools and colleges, in his plays and shows, in parades and pageants, in his work place and bedroom. The Rulers successfully manufacture a sufficient quantity of cannon fodder, glorious killers, and morally confused creatures, ready to perform any unholy deed they are ordered.

In these and other ways, the Executioners and the Executives of History successfully pervert and demoralize the humanity of our age. They do this job more successfully than the Tempter of Jesus did. They outdevil the Devil himself.

Such are the blasphemies of the poisonous "idiots of unselfish love."

The idiots assert further that You, the Guardians of the World Order and the World Holiness, are the *stranglers of the spirit of Creativity, its falsifiers and misusers.*

They say that Your dungeons are Your temples, that the places of execution of Your enemies are Your Holy of Holies. The dungeons' dark caverns and the places of execution have witnessed thousands of creators, great and small, imprisoned, tortured, poisoned, decapitated, hanged, shot, crucified, guillotined, and murdered in other torturous ways. By Your order Socrates had to drink the deadly hemlock. You crucified Jesus. You crucified and quartered Al Hallaj. You murdered Servetus. You tortured and condemned to death the Apostles, and more than a third of all the Christian saints. You guillotined Lavoisier and killed Condorcet, burned Joan of Arc and murdered thousands of creators in science and religion, philosophy and ethics, fine arts and technology, economics and politics.

Hundreds of thousands of other creators have been imprisned, banished, tortured, deprived of their rights and privileges and in many other ways persecuted by You. You sold into slavery Plato; from You Confucius, Lao-Tse, and Aristotle had to flee to save their lives. You banished Dante, arrested St. Thomas Aquinas, ostracized Hobbes, threatened the life of Rousseau. In many ingenious ways You persecuted hundreds of thousands, nay, millions, of creators.

Especially merciless and deadly is Your persecution of genius and talent at the present time. The Upstart Rulers of the Russian, Fascist, Nazi, Spanish, and Chinese revolutions alone have murdered thousands of great creators and tens of thousands of smaller talents. These Executioners of History have imprisoned, tortured, banished and otherwise persecuted hundreds of thousands of creators. In a smaller degree the same is true of the contemporary Legitimate Rulers. Their hands are also dripping with the blood of their creative victims. They are responsible also for many suicides of the hunted-down "subversives," and for a milder persecution of their brainy opponents. Especially murderous are the myrmidons of the Big Lords. If the Great Rulers themselves are envious of the Holy Creative Spirit and cannot easily co-exist with its human instrumentalities, the uncreative myrmidons cannot tolerate at all any genius, any talent, anybody marked by the grace of creativity. For this reason alone, these bullies oppress and suppress the Free Spirit of Creativity anywhere and at any time they have a chance. These myrmidons function as members of the secret and open police, as little judges and politicians, as members of various Committees on Un-Committees Activities, as members of various pseudo-military cohorts, as loyal superpatriots, and as the lilliputian Daughters and Sons of Great Ancestors.

The pacifistic runts add to this that the Upstart and the Legitimate Rulers persecute genius and talent in many other forms: by discriminating against them and favoring the sterile yes-men and yes-women; by demoting the independent creators and by promoting the uncreative eunuchs; and so on.

In these ways the ruling caste has murdered, stunned, hindered, and crushed an uncounted multitude of potential and actual creators. In the opinion of the lunatic runts, there is hardly any other social group or other force as disastrous in this respect as are You, the Mighty Giants of Power and Glory.

Our Majestic Enormities! The crazy gnats of peace go further in their accusations. Besides the extermination of genius and talent, You are guilty, in their opinion, of the misuse of their creative achievements. Faithfully serving Your Master, the Unholy Killer and Perverter, You try to use scientific discoveries for destructive purposes, ideological systems for propagation of hate, artistic achievements for the ugliest ends. The brilliant discoveries of subatomic physics You have turned into Satanic bombs, the findings of bacteriology into bacteriological warfare, and those of chemistry and technology into horrible gadgets of mass murder. If the misuse of "the tree of knowledge" at the dawn of history cost humanity its Garden of Eden, Your misuse of science and philosophy, technology and the fine arts, ethics and economics now threatens the very tree of human life. Instead of using creativity to the greater glory of God and the nobler improvements of man, You use it for death and destruction. Instead of leaving genius free to serve the God of creation, You force it to work for Your Unholy Master. In this way You desecrate the Truth, the Goodness, and the Beauty. Serving Your Master, You sacrilegiously disserve the Infinite Creative Soul of the Universe. Only the All-merciful Creator can forgive Your mortal sin against the Holy Creative Spirit! Pray for this forgiveness and stop Your sacrilege!

Finally, the perverted morons of forgiveness and peace accuse You, the Preservers and Builders of Nations, of bleeding to death your faithful flocks, in selective killing of the fittest and the best, and in helping the survival of the least fit in Your nations. You draft into Your armies the best youth of Your nations — the best physically, vitally, mentally, and morally. Then You kill this best youth in Your endless wars and bloodsheds. The sick, the defective, the moronish, and the criminal among the youth are exempt from Your draft. They are left to procreate and replenish the earth. This policy of Yours squanders the best blood and leads Your nations to eventual degeneration.

Your persecution of genius and extermination of talents greatly facilitates this impoverishment. Taken together, Your policies are the surest way to the physical, vital, mental, and moral decay of Your faithful flocks. Here again You serve well Your Unholy Master, the Great Killer, Destroyer, and Perverter.

Such are the mad laments and the berserk accusations of the idiots of peace against You, Our Blameless Lords and Protectors. Mercifully forgive us, Your devout servants, for reporting these blasphemies to You. Now that we have done our duty, we pray to You for Your help in our struggle with the berserkers. Enlighten us with Your crushing answers to their accusations. Let Your just punishment fall upon the impious rebels! Let their poisonous tongues be cut off. If this is not enough to stop their destructive activities, let their lives be ended and their seed be exterminated from this planet. Cleared from all the lunatics of the "love thine enemies," from all the rebellious creators, the earth will regain its eternal peace under Your wise guidance. Praise be the Lords of the Human Universe!

Devout Complaints to the Keepers of Our Souls

Our Spiritual Fathers! The Guardians of Our Souls! The Guides of Our Salvation! We, Your spiritual children, are confused and lost in the darkness of the moral jungle of our time. We do not know which of its trails are right and which are wrong, which lead to the bottomless pit of perdition and which lead to the sunny, fertile and beautiful valley. Many a time we humbly asked for Your unerring advice and for Your spiritual help. Each time You have kindly granted it. But Your generosity has somehow failed to aid us in our mortal plight. The fault of the failure is, of course, entirely ours. To our deaf ears Your unerring councils often sounded as mere mumbling without any clear meaning. At other times, Your advice appeared to our ignorant minds as self-contradictory. Sometimes it looked contradictory even to the Sacred Scripture and to the Word of God You profess. Now and then Your magnificent sermons sounded to our brainlessness as a mere pouring of emptiness into vacuum and vacuum into emptiness. On other occasions, in Your holy rolling, in Your violent convulsions, and Your endlessly repeated yelling at the top of Your voice, "Our Lord, the Savior," "Our Jesus or Buddha," "Our Allah or Brahma," You looked like madhouse patients. Once in a while the pomp and ostentation, colorfulness and brilliancy of Your ritualistic pageants have been overwhelming. All this magnificent variety has not, however, cleared our bewilderment.

Our confusion is greatly increased by the denunciation of the lunatics of peace and the fanatics of meekness. These maniacs are raving against You, *Patres Spirituales,* no less than against all the "upper-upper" and the "upper-middle" and the "upper-lower" leaders of mankind. Now and then they rave even against the "middle-upper" and the "lower-middle" strata of the social pyramid.

Your own conduct also contributes to our stupefaction. Often we are stunned by it and cannot understand its why and wherefore. We firmly believe that you, Monopolistic Confidantes and Intimate Secretaries of the Heavenly Unmoved Mover, know everything about Him — even such details as that He has not revised the Hindu or the Hebrew editions of His Scripture for some three thousand years while the Christian edition of His Scripture has not been revised by Him for some two thousand years. We know well that what in Your preaching and practice appears to us unscrutable has a superhuman meaning and a divine reason. Trusting You unconditionally, for the sake of salvation of our souls from eternal damnation, we earnestly pray You, the Ambassadors of the Heavenly Powers, to dissipate our moral darkness and to guide us from the dangerous jungles to the promised land of spiritual milk rivers flowing between material ice-cream banks.

Plenipotentiaries of the Stratospheric Lights! Our ignorant

minds, if we have minds at all, do not comprehend the teachings of some of Your most Eminent Luminaries. These Stars preach that neither Jesus nor Buddha, neither Lao-Tse nor Confucius, neither Moses nor Mahavira took their moral teachings seriously. The Luminaries of the Theological Skies learnedly prove that Jesus never meant His Sermon on the Mount to be practiced by His followers.

"Jesus was not so stupid as not to understand the super-human character of His rules of conduct. He issued His commandments playfully, just for fun, as a fanciful dream of the young Son of God." The Luminaries logically conclude that the true followers of Jesus — or Buddha — are neither expected nor obliged to live according to His precepts. They can sin as much as they please and at the same time call themselves true Christians. They can parade the Sermon on the Mount in their business advertising or in mass murder or sex affairs; and at the same time, incessantly violate it in their actual practice. The doctrine of these Sacred Doctors is marvelous indeed. It permits everyone to enjoy all the sins he commits and in spite of this, be fully saved. It buys for nothing the Halo of Christian Saintliness and the whole Kingdom of God. Of all kinds of bargains ever offered on all kinds of markets, there has hardly ever been such a profitable offer. Even we, ignorant folk, understand why so many millions are grabbing the bargain, especially those who sin and enjoy their sins fully. Without any payment or diet it guarantees a big mansion in the Kingdom to Come.

And yet, Our Preaching Sonorities, other Angelic Doctors tell us that the bargain doctrine is all crooked and does not buy any place in the Kingdom of Good Jesus. Nor does it correctly interpret the moral teachings of the Son of God. If anything, it contradicts them and distorts them and turns them into a seductive profanity of the Great Perverter. If not by our little reason, then by our horse sense we feel that the Luminaries misinterpret our Good Jesus and His Divine Message of Love. By this distortion they prepare the ground for an infinitely greater falsification — a substitution of the Destroyer's lies for the Glad Tidings of the Son of God. In the name of Jesus they consecrate the horrible misdeeds of the Unholy. In the place of Christ they are enthroning Antichrist himself.

Ministers of Our Souls! We are appalled at these suspicions and forebodings. We are horrified at the possibility of an unjust accusation of Our Spiritual Fathers in this mortal sin. And yet, the preachings and the deeds of many of You seem to confirm our suspicions. The lunatics of "love thine enemy" are absolutely certain about that. They accuse You, the Unerring Experts of the Heavenly Mystery, of daily crucifying Jesus and indefatigably repudiating His teachings.

You crucify Him when You preach a murderous crusade against the alleged enemies of God and Jesus. You crucify Him when you pray to Jesus for help in the mass murder of all Your opponents. You repudiate Jesus when You bless the murderous arms to be successful in their murderous effects. You replace Jesus by the Great Killer when You substitute the message of deadly, poisonous hate for the glad tidings of all-giving and all-forgiving love: love of God to man, of man to God, and of man to man and to every creature in the universe.

You repudiate Jesus each time You preach Your doctrine of the *tribal* God. You falsify His message of brotherhood by Your tribal pseudo-brotherhood of distribution of medals mainly among the Powers of This World. You falsify the ethics of Jesus by a phony moral rearmament.

You repudiate Jesus each time You fail to raise Your voice against any act of hate, any bloodshed, any violence, any injustice, any exploitation.

You repudiate Jesus each time You fail to drive out of the

Sacred Temple of the Highest Values all the merchants who turn it into a profane black market and all the killers who make out of it a den of gangsters.

You reject Jesus each time, when, for motives of cowardice or profit, You fail to denounce the unholy crimes of all the Ruling Powers, of all the Mighty and the Rich, and of all the agents of the Great Killer.

You serve Mammon and not God when for temporary profit You "sensibly" preach the effortless, emotionally thrilling and carnally pleasing doctrine of salvation by a mere monotonous repetition of a few magical words or by mere attendance at Sunday's ritualistic pageants or by catering to the High Hierarchy of the Secular and the Spiritual Powers.

In Your crucifixion of Jesus You have gone so far that in His name You dare to approve shamelessly even the use of atom bombs, to bless the bloodiest wars, and to invoke blasphemously the name of God for consecration of the vilest actions of the Destroyer.

Your defection from and blasphemy against Jesus and God has progressed so far that if Jesus would appear again among us and would start His mission anew, You would declare Him the most dangerous subversive, denounce Him to the Committees on Un-Committees Activities and eventually would crucify Him again.

We are sick, the lunatics say, with Your hypocrisy, with Your spiritual cowardice, with Your subservience to the Mighty Powers of this world, with Your distortion of the great moral teachings, with Your forgeries and falsifications — even with Your clumsy subterfuges to marry science with religion, Freud with Jesus, and Hell with Heaven.

Neither You, False Experts of Salvation, nor we, the foolish followers of the Sermon on the Mount, are surprised at the rapid waning of Your authority, influence, and even social position. Trying to prepare simultaneously a comfortable house in this world and a mansion in the World to Come, You fail in both endeavors. "If the salt have lost his savor, wherewith shall it be salted? It is thenceforth good for nothing but to be cast out, and to be trodden under foot of men."

We, Your spiritual children, do not share the raving of the lunatics. But we feel that in a small part their denunciations are true. We pray to Jesus that He mercifully send His true missionaries to reconvert to Christianity all the false Christian Ministers and Spiritual Guides. They need the true missionaries more than the pagans. We pray to God that He enlighten the Spiritual Fathers of other great religions: Judaism and Mohammedanism, Confucianism and Taoism, Hinduism and Buddhism, atheism and materialism, and the hundreds of small sects and religious currents of our days. We all are lost in the bloody darkness of our days. We all need the Enlightenment by the All-merciful Soul of the World. Once more, we need the Lamb of God to take upon Himself our mortal sins. Good, Loving, Kind Jesus. Have your inexhaustible mercy upon us!

NAIVE QUERIES OF SIMPLETONS TO THE MAGICIANS OF SCIENCE, THE MIRACLE-MAKERS OF TECHNOLOGY, AND TO THE TESTOLOGISTS AND WORD-WEAVERS OF SCHOLARSHIP

Proud Descendants of Prometheus! Learned Weavers of Words into Meaningless Carpets! Exactest Psychometricians, Sociometricians, and Econometricians precisely measuring the Immeasurables! And You, Manufacturers of Psychosocial Tests Testing Nobody Knows What!

You successfully stole the secrets of Zeus and of other deities! You unraveled the deepest mysteries of the State Department of Nature: You out-F.B.I.ed the F.B.I. itself. You overthrew the

obsolescent gods and goddesses. You undermined the aristoc-
racies of the ancient past, the *nouveaux riches,* and the proletarians of the present.

You rightfully enthroned Your Scientific Luminosities and
Your Scholarly Incandescences in the place of gods and aristoc-
racies. You made Yourselves the leaders of the bourgeoisie and
the proletariat. You are absolutely indispensable even for the
Upstart and the Legitimate Rulers. Without Your help they
cannot have either power or dictatorship. Your Scientific Omni-
potences! Your power is boundless. You produce rain out of
drought and drought out of wetness. You turn the Arctic into
the Tropics, and vice versa. By Your fingertip You can explode
this poor planet into nothingness. And by a mere twinkling of
Your eye You can turn us, the simpletons, into a mere sub-sub-
sub-atomic myth.

Your Scholastic Resplendencies! Your erudition and word-
polishing are wonderful. Your historical, philosophical, political, economic, sociological, and psychological researches are
astounding. The footnotes on footnotes, the annotations on annotations, the quotations on quotations, the single-, plural-, par-
allel-, diagonal-, and criss-cross references in Your treatises are
stupefying.

Still more incomprehensible are the measurements of Your
Metromaniacs, the objective tests of Your Testophreniacs, and
"the techniques of psychosocial research" of Your Technomaniacs. Only Omniscient God can possibly understand how the
Metromaniacs can measure the relationships between various
sociocultural immeasurables and especially between the incom-
mensurable immeasurable variables. Only the Pythias of psychology, the Oracles of psychiatry, and the Clairvoyants of socio-
anthropology can unravel the mysteries of the mass-manufactured
tests: mental and intelligence tests, the aptitude tests, the Ror-

schach tests, the tea-leaves tests, the cloud-formation tests, the card tests, the Mortimer Snerd and Charlie McCarthy tests, and the thousands of other tests, one more mysterious than the other, up to the supermysterious tests of loyalty and subversivity. We mortals cannot understand either the reasons of a given test, or what it tests, or what the testing results mean. All this transcends our mortal capacity and demands the extraordinary wisdom of the inhabitants of insane asylums, of Doctors I.Q. of Radio Entertainment, and of the infallible intuition of members of Loyalty Boards.

As to the techniques of the Psychosocial Technomaniacs, their inventions and discoveries are truly epoch-making. Each day they discover America by the newly invented technique of crossing the Atlantic on the *Queen Elizabeth* or the *Ile de France*. By other new techniques, they discover either the great uniformity of seasonal sequence — that after the spring comes the summer, then the autumn, and then the winter; or that two and two make four. Sometimes, however, when they use a particularly precise technique, they find that two plus two make exactly 3.367291, plus-minus .0000065. With the help of the big Research Foundations now and then they set forth very great research projects studying particularly important causal relationships and casual correlations between the most strategic variables like the number of spittings and the number of leaves on the trees in a given city; the number of fire engines and the church attendance; the secular trends in the number of touchdowns in the football games of the season, and in the number of screwballs born in the country. These and other basic problems of the social and humanistic sciences they study with the marvelous techniques of anti-mathematical statistics, anti-logical semantics, anti-observational psychoanalysis, anti-rational operationalism, and by the techniques of the thoughtlessly nondirective interviewing, of the open-and-closed interrogation, of the guided-in-unguided questionnaires of the clinical psychologists, sociologists, and anthropologists.

These measuring procedures, testing devices, and technical operations of Yours, Our Scholarly Non-Mystical Mist-Makers, transcend not only our primitive intelligence but even the gigantic brains of the starry mathematicians, physicists, logicians and biologists. They also do not understand Your homemade supra-mathematics, para-testology, and meta-techniques.

Now that we, ignoramuses, have paid our profound homage to Your Scientific Might and Scholarly Glory, may we be permitted respectfully to ask You, the Enlighteners of the Darkness, a few questions?

We know that You regard Yourselves and Your Science high above and far beyond the subjective notions of right and wrong, bad and good, beautiful and ugly, healthy and deadly. You never fail to re-re-re-repeat to us that science is objective and perfectly indifferent to all of these arbitrary evaluations. Even our feeble brains can remember this after so many restatements.

If science is indifferent, and can equally serve Life and Death, Peace and War, the Unholy Destroyers and the God of Creation, why then have You and Your Science not consistently served only Life, Peace, and Creativity? Why, instead, have You often served Death, War, and Destruction? Through Your deadly "tree of knowledge" mankind lost his Garden of Eden at the dawn of history; and since that time, science and scholarship have often contributed enormously to the Great Destroyer. If, as scientists and scholars, You are morally and socially irresponsible, as human beings, You *are* responsible for what You and Your Science do to Your fellow men and the human universe of values. As human beings should not You be vitally interested in building rather than in destroying, in living rather than dying, in being happy rather than in suffering, in serving

Truth, Beauty, and Love rather than Error, Ugliness, and Hate? Indifference means an equal easiness in serving either one of these two Opposite Values. Why then, have You and Your Science so often sinned by serving the Unholy instead of the Holy? Is it Your cussedness or Your stupidity that is responsible for these scientific crimes of Yours against humanity, life, and the Creator?

Why is Your scientific service to the Great Destroyer especially active at the present time? Why do almost all of Your brainiest scientists and scholars serve now mainly the Satan of Destruction and the Great Killer?

Why are all Your energies devoted now to the invention of the deadliest means of destruction? Why are You so anxious to kill mankind and all the life on this planet? Why do You want to turn the planet itself into a mere puff? What is the reason for this scientific madness of Yours?

You cannot plead ignorance of what You are doing because better than anyone else You understand the irrevocable catastrophe You are preparing. You know well that millions of human beings are already killed by Your inventions and that hundreds of millions are going to be murdered tomorrow.

You realize fully that among the gang of the murderers of these millions already slaughtered and those to be murdered tomorrow, You are the chief murderer. Without Your brains the Rulers, their myrmidons, and the masses could never invent these destructive means; they would have had to be satisfied with slaughter on a much smaller scale.

If we hold responsible for manslaughter a car driver who, without any intention, inadvertently runs over a child and kills him, how much more responsible are You for these mass murders? In comparison with You, the worst murderer is almost a saint. He kills only one or a few persons and kills often through his ignorance, stupidity, or misery. You kill millions coldbloodedly and You have none of these extenuating circumstances. Why then are You doing this Unholy and Ugly crime against all laws, divine and human — against all moral precepts, against any decency, even against Your own interests and life? Killing others now, You eventually will kill also Yourselves.

Do You do this because the Rulers want it? Are you the caterers to all the crazy wishes of the Rulers? Do You not have Your own standards of right and wrong? And is not a slavish catering to the whims of all sorts of politicians incompatible with science and the dignity of Scientists and Scholars? Since when did You become mere lackeys of the Cynical Potentates?

Do You do this because the Rulers command You? No criminal command is binding and no command excuses any crime of anyone, especially the most horrible crime against humanity and God.

Do You do this because otherwise You might be penalized? There have been and there always will be many a martyr who may have been penalized by capital punishment for discharge of his moral duty. But he prefers to fulfill his duty regardless of the consequences. Why should You be an exception to the moral imperative, obligatory for all? Don't You ordinarily claim that You are not only the intellectual but also the moral salt of the earth? In addition, in most cases no serious penalty threatens You for Your refusal to participate in the murderous inventions.

Is it the promise of good salary, fame, and the chance to do scientific research? Even ordinary criminals rarely try to justify their crimes by this argument of a weak sister. None of these "boons" can acquit even a pickpocket. Still less can they annul the greatest crime against humanity and science itself.

None of these reasons can justify Your appalling service to the Great Killer and the Unholy Destroyer.

Your sin becomes grotesque when, doing it, You begin simultaneously to plead for moderation in the use of Your inventions and respectfully petition the Rulers to use them only in an emergency and not too liberally. In Your whining You resemble young pups who, after wetting mischief, begin to whine and apologetically crawl on all fours, asking for pardon. What is funny in the pups is disgusting in the proud heirs of Prometheus. By Your "humanitarian" whining You lose the last vestige of Your dignity and glamour. Better be unrepentant sinners than hypocritical whiners.

Scholarly Vibrators of Air Waves and Processers of Paper! Voracious Book-Eaters! Metromaniacs, Testophreniacs, and Technomaniacs of Psychosocial Sciences! You of course are not guilty of these sins of the natural scientist — not by Your virtue but by Your impotence, for one cannot explode a planet by the slight vibration of air in Your incessant talks, or by the wasting of paper in Your indefatigable writings, or by the feverish testing of nobody knows what, and for what.

But You also serve the Great Killer in Your own way, first, as the ideological parasites of the bloodsucking parasites of humanity. While the mighty and the exploiters directly suck the blood of the ruled and the exploited, You get Your living as parasitic servants of the bloodsuckers. In this sense You are the vegetarian suckers of the carnivorous leeches of humanity.

You serve the Unholy Killer as his ideologists. Like Your teacher, Machiavelli, You glorify wars and murders, beautify brigandage and treachery, idealize perfidy and forgery, ennoble brutality and sensuality in all forms. Your ideologies whitewash the blood of the Killer's victims, deodorize the stench of their corpses, and drown the cries of agony in the deadening music of the marches militaires and factional anthems.

You serve the Great Perverter by confusing our minds and consciences. You serve the Unholy by grinding all values into dust, by uglifying the beautiful, and ignobling the noble, by mortalizing the immortal, and by dragging all values into the social sewers. Your ideologies demoralize and stultify us, poor simpletons. For this reason, perhaps, Lao-Tse said that scholars are never wise and wise men are never scholars. Having passed through Your educational procedures, we emerge from them as human derelicts, rather than integrated persons reverently walking the earth and proudly looking into the starry heaven.

You are supposed to be our educators, our civic and cultural leaders and the sterling example for our imitation. Where are You in these times of saturated catastrophy? Why do we not hear Your clear voice, and hear instead only Your mumblings? What shining example of wisdom, courage, and impeccable virtue do You set for us to imitate and follow? What road do You advise us to take to reach the Promised Land? Alas! These quests of ours remain either unanswered or they are answered in the most depressing way.

Instead of heroic courage we see only Your subservience to Your immediate bosses — the henchmen of the Great Killer. In place of wisdom You mumble: "Do what your bosses wish and you shall be safe, prosperous, and successful." In lieu of the moral imperative "Thou shalt not kill," You indefatigably preach: "To kill and to be killed by the order of the bosses is your supreme duty" . . . "only the successful killers survive in the struggle for existence" . . . "killing is the universal law of life" . . . "the greatest good of our time is to strike first and kill millions of innocent persons before you are slaughtered among the millions of guiltless humans."

You never fail to praise this "man eat man" moral of the Great Killer and accordingly organize the whole system of education from the cradle to the grave. From his earliest days, You surround every child with murderous toys — guns, swords, bombs, knives — and teach him how to kill the enemies, how to torture them, how to deceive them, how to do all sorts of possible harm.

You skillfully instill into Your pupils the ideals of cutthroat competition, unmitigated rivalry, and the merciless: "business is business" like "war is war." All this is inculcated in the framework of the exclusive tribalism: "If I harm somebody it is good; if he harms me, it is bad."

In order to make these activities easy, You train Your students in the art of sincere hypocrisy, artful lying, and artistic deceit. Your ideologies and techniques are cut out accordingly. They vary in accordance with the sex, age, race, intelligence, social status, and culture of the students, but their main objectives remain the same: the education for killing and being killed.

In pursuit of this end, in these trying times, Your leaders, the presidents of the great universities and colleges, of the academies of science and arts, of the national and international educational associations, have especially distinguished themselves. In their enlightened enthusiasm they outrival even the professional myrmidons of the Great Killer. The great educators not only approve the drafting of the young blood of the nations for death, but they generously demand an increase of the quota to the highest possible limit: to fight up to the last youth of humanity. And the age limits of the drafted youth they try to progressively lower, down to the lowest possible age. "The younger the better": such is their humanitarian motto.

Having made a bloody mess of their own lives and the whole human universe, the great educators and the old people are most enthusiastic to clear the mess by sacrificing all the young blood of humanity to the Great Moloch. In contrast to Jesus, in their interpretation "the greatest love" consists not in giving their own lives for the lives of the innocent youth, but in taking the lives of the youth in payment for their own sins and the sins of the old-aged groups — a wonderful improvement upon the naive statement of an uneducated Jesus!

We, the simpletons, are too ignorant to understand the

wisdom of Your policies of war and peace. To our poor minds, if our leaders cannot live without war, they themselves should be drafted first, and fight it out among themselves. We agree with Leo Tolstoy on this point:

Leave us alone. If you, emperors, generals, judges, bishops, professors, if you have need of armies, navies, courts, prisons, gallows, guillotines, prepare them all yourselves; tax yourselves, judge yourselves, imprison and execute yourselves, get yourselves killed in war; but leave us alone, for we have no need of all these things and we do not wish to participate in acts that are so futile and above all, so wicked.

Let the Politburo of the Kremlin and the Rulers of the Atlantic Union draft themselves and, if they wish, fight each other. If additional drafts are to be made, then the remaining members of the ruling groups are to be called to the colors, then persons of sixty and over, then fifty and over, and so on. The youth below twenty years of age should not be drafted at all or be drafted the last. Since international messes are created by the governments and the old-age groups, since it is the governments who start wars and bloodshed, since the old-age groups already have lived almost the whole span of their lives and have had all the chance to display their creative potential, it does not make much difference for them whether they are killed now or would die a few years later. For these reasons, the governments and the old people should be the first to be drafted and be sent to the battlefield. In contrast to them, the youth did not create the international mess, youth is not responsible for all the tensions and hatred; they have not lived even one third of a normal human life, and have not had a chance to show their creative potential. The reasons of justice, wisdom, and of survival of mankind all demand leaving the youth at peace, out of all drafts and wars, because only the youth can clean up the mess of their fathers and can build a new, harmonious, and beautiful human universe.

Educational Excellencies and Scholastic Highnesses! We bring our humblest apology for these ignorant notions of ours. To Your Educated Wisdom these notions probably appear mis-educational and stupid. We dare not disagree with Your verdict. The reason for our stupidity is possibly an insufficiency of the education You have given to us. By Your generous effort it has to be replenished and completed. Then our notions would be exact replicas of Yours; our policies would duplicate Your wise policies; and we ourselves would turn into third-class parrots of Your Educational Brightnesses and Your Scholastic Profundities. We pray You to help us in this pious wish of ours. Otherwise, we are bound to entertain various silly notions and live in darkness. Let the magical efficiency of Your scientific techniques vacuum clean our undeveloped minds of all the dust of our ignorance; let Your educational pumps fill us with Your scientific and scholastic presumptions, assumptions, reservations, qualifications, hypotheses, approximations, conditions, virtualities of the subconscious, unconscious, and conscious drives and instincts, of unconditional, conditional, and prepotent reflexes, of mysterious ids, egos and superegos. Armed with all these instruments of scholastic education, we shall certainly know more and more about less and less, everything about nothing, and nothing about everything. So transfigured, we shall be admitted into Your Kingdom of misleading preciseness, trained incapacity, and qualified ignorance. Amen.

ENTREATIES OF HUMAN COGS TO THE MASTODONS OF INDUSTRY, ELEPHANTS OF FINANCE, LIONS OF LABOR, AND ELKS OF AGRICULTURE

Now we turn our prayers to You, the Demiurges of Wealth, the Producers of Bread and Butter, the Manufacturers of Cars and Atomic Bombs, the Gigantic Backseat Drivers of the Mechanical Frankensteins in whose endless wheels we, human cogs, are hopelessly enmeshed and ground to dust. Give us this day our daily bread and forgive us our trespasses against You, regardless of whether it is You who trample us under Your mighty feet or it is we who unfortunately happen to impede the free motions of Your mastodonic paws. In either case and in any case, it is not You, but we, the cogs, who are always guilty and need Your magnanimous pardon.

We know well that without Your managerial, working, and unionizing activities of production of everything out of nothing, the whole world of material commodities would never have been born. The arrogant materialistic ideologists, beginning with Democritus and Lucretius and ending with Karl Marx and Lenin are but mere idealistic pups in comparison with Your Elephantine Material Substantiality. Their materialistic ideologies are but an ideational refraction of the solid materiality of Your making; they are mere thin air in comparison with the world of steel and reinforced concrete, of gold and platinum, of oil and uranium, of everything-crushing machines and everything-building gadgets created by You. Instead of angry barking at You, these pups should crawl before You on all fours. Without You, they would have nobody to bark at, and no way to gratify themselves with their materialistic delusions. Without the material world of Your creation, no materialistic ideology would even occur to the ingrates' abnormal brains. They truly deserve a good whipping!

Without Your organizational activity we would remain an unorganized mob of roving human animals. Without Your managerial regimentation we would not be able to produce anything, even bread and water to keep our souls and bodies together. Without Your unionizing cement we would remain human dust blown hither and thither by all the winds of bad fortune. With Your leadership we are united into interminable rows of cogwheels, running round and round in a repetition of the same little motion day in, day out, to the end of our lives in Your Frankensteins of mass production. You have unified us so perfectly and made our lives so marvelous that no brains, no soul, and no will on our part is necessary to run the life-cycle of a human cog. You have arranged our lives so well that we, cogs, are quite satisfied with the lot You have prepared for us. Your wisdom has dictated that our lot, like that of Your working cattle, should be "not too much and not too little, just the golden mean below the equilibrium point" — enough to keep us from starvation and complete ignorance, but not enough to permit development of sinful pride, pernicious independence, and especially of the soul striving to soar *per aspera ad astra*. The soul in cogs is scientific nonsense, philosophical absurdity, moral sin, religious sacrilege, and economic disaster.

We are grateful to You for allotting to us a chance to live the normal span of a shortened human life, and to die without being murdered by or murdering somebody. We are still more thankful to You for making our lives not only automatic but also full and meaningful. You generously enrich it by a proper quota of the *Daily Bleached News* and the *Digest of Digests of All the Digests* for our mental growth; of the best band-jazz-crooning music for our aesthetic culture; of football-baseball-screwball for our sport development; of horse-dog-cow races for our thrills; of movies, championship fights, and night clubs for our emotional maturity; of necking-spooning-dating for our sex refinement; of radio soap operas, television comedies, and comic books for our entertainment. Our words are insufficient rightly to describe all the fullness, refinement, and significance of our cog-life tailored by You, Planners and Molders of our subconscious libido, conscious ego, and standardized superego. With the help of Your psychoanalytic experts, You have ad-

justed us to the life of cogs and sublimated to it our bodies and
the atavistic remains of our former souls, Glory to You for this
magnanimous miracle!

Our only worry is that this adjustment seems to be not quite
perfect as yet. Now and then the automatic equilibrium of
our lives is still being disturbed by various squalls of brooding,
grudges, doubts, questions, and fear. All this is very likely due
to the incompleteness of the extinction of our atavistic soul and
to its quests, anxieties, and especially to its morbid aspirations
for a non-automatic life, free creativity, and mystical spirituality.
Whatever the reasons, the worries and uncomfortable questions
continue to pester us.

For instance, we often wonder why, in contrast to Your great
ancestors who favored the development of the culture of Shake-
speares and Beethovens, of Rembrandts and Michelangelos, of
Erasmuses and Kants, of Tolstois and Balzacs, of Mark Twains
and Melvilles, now You sponsor mainly the culture of the
voiceless voices, incessantly crooning on all radios, of musically
deaf bandleaders impudently jazzing Bach and Beethoven, of
a crowd of comedians tirelessly repeating the same jokes as dull
as last year's razor blade — the culture of standardized and rub-
ber-stamped murder stories, mystery stories, sex adventures and
sex confessions? Why do You so enthusiastically sponsor the
ugliest light-medium-heavyweight fights? Why do You de-
liberately support and finance the most vulgar dailies and magazines, the most incompetent columnists, irresponsible commentators, and tasteless critics? Why do You feed us with
the worst possible kind of movies and plays? Why do You
glamorize the ugliest crimes and perversions? Why do You
glorify the dirtiest, the most pathological, and the shadiest
aspects of our lives? Why do You drag all values into the social
sewers and drown them there? In brief, why do You try to
destroy the great cultural achievements of Your and our an-

cestors and to replace them with what Your enemies call the most vulgar, the ugliest, and the least creative pseudo-culture of the Decadent Social Sewer Man? And how much worse is this Social Sewer Man that You have developed, say Your critics, than prehistoric Caveman? What was created by the efforts of many geniuses for many generations, our Captains of Industry and Finance, assisted by Labor Leaders, successfully destroy within one generation. What marvellous efficiency!

These accusations are probably wrong, but the remnants of our atavistic souls do not allow us to pass them by undisturbed. Somehow or other they are bothering us. Will You and Your psychoanalytical experts help us in this matter?

Another thing that bothers us is Your business efficiency and indefatigable dynamism. You proudly call Yourselves business-men and You justly prefer this title to any other title in the world. In contrast to the Great Creator who, we are told, after six days of creation rested, and looked and enjoyed His creation, You never rest and never enjoy the results of Your business activity. You cannot even relax, because relaxation means a lower efficiency which is, in Your ethical code, a mortal sin.

We would not mind Your cult of efficiency if You were not imposing it also upon us, the cogs. Imposing it on us, You de-prive us of the few moments of relaxation, of luxurious laziness, the *dolce far niente,* which You Yourselves reserved for us in Your "plan of the life-cycle of the industrial cogs." We would not mind it if Your or our feverish business motility would always yield good results. Your critics claim, however, that Your and our incessant running is no more productive than the endless running of a squirrel in a cage. The critics dug out somewhere the crazy statement of the old Chinese lunatic Lao-Tse that "doing nothing is better than to be busy doing nothing." In the critics' opinion You are madly busy doing nothing either creative or valuable or even pleasurable. Your cult of efficiency

leads all of us only to nervous breakdowns, heart failures, and
premature death. The Chinese lunatic and the critics are, of
course, wrong. But we cannot help being bothered by the
cult of being busy doing nothing. Will You and Your psychiatrists free us from all this anxiety?

Our Busy Masters! There are other neurotic quests that worry
us. They, too, are probably the survival effects of the remnants
of our former soul still smoldering somewhere between our libido,
ego, and superego. These worries are Your unquenchable passion for unlimited wealth and power; Your insatiable competition
for the sake of competition and for having more than the others
have; and finally, Your enthusiasm for war as the supreme form
of rivalry. To our standardized mind You already have all the
power and all the wealth one can wish. Your fortune is so great
that the kings are but beggars in comparison with You. The
same is true of Your power. Many governments are but the
figureheads moved by Your little finger. We cannot understand
why You are not satisfied with what You have, why You want
to grab still more.

"Wealth-Competition-Efficiency" is Your answer to these questions. This is Your modern formula for the old-fashioned Trinity. In Your Credo this new Trinity rules the world. Efficient
competition for wealth is the ultimate force that moves the
world and keeps it busy. Wealth as a sort of God Father is the
primary source of everything valuable and real. Without it
nothing can exist and be tangible. Without competition nothing
valuable can be created or be redeemed and exchanged. Without
competition the world itself could neither be born nor function
well. Finally, efficiency is Your new "Holy Ghost" emanating
from the Father-Wealth and the Son-Competition. Where this
Trinity operates, there is business, prosperity, and life. Where
efficient competition for wealth is lacking, there is misery, stagnation, and life-in-death. Such is Your Credo.

As invincible evidence of its validity, You point at Buddha, Socrates, Lao-Tse, Jesus, St. Francis, Mozart, Beethoven, Gandhi, and thousands of other disbelievers. "Look what a mess these defamers of competition made out of their lives and how miserably they ended their existence. They did not believe in the all-curing and all-creating power of competition. Instead they extolled love, mutual aid, and sacrifice. No wonder they lived so wretchedly and ended their lives so disgracefully: either as criminals they were condemned to death, like Socrates and Jesus, or, like Gandhi, they were murdered by the believers in competition; or, like St. Francis and Mozart, they lived and died as paupers; or, like Lao-Tse and Buddha, they became tramps and eventually faded away. And if such is the lot of these big detractors of competition, still more miserable is the lot of the small disbelievers. Any nation that neglects competition is doomed to perdition. Each nation that shares our Credo becomes ever bigger and better." Such is Your further answer to our quests as well as to Your critics.

This brilliant philosophy naturally leads You, the Dynamos of Efficiency, to the glorification of war as the supreme competition. As builders of the gigantic arsenal of destruction and death, dictators of production and distribution, of prices and wages, of life, behavior, relationships of the citizens, and as the real movers of war, kings, presidents, dictators, generals, and admirals; as harvesters of war profits, You find in war a gigantic elemental force congenial to Your own dynamic genius. You love war as the superhuman challenge to Your superman's capacity for domination. Being arch-gamblers You enjoy the reckless war gamble of either winning or losing everything. Especially when the losing everything means somebody else. We respect Your romantic passion for war and its real motives. They are highly idealistic and have little to do with greediness, profit, and other prosaic reasons.

And yet, we are still not entirely free from an anxiety complex in these matters. We cannot logically repudiate Your Credo and especially Your crucial argument about the just retribution of all detractors of Your Trinity. Our minds, standardized slightly above the borderline intelligence, simply cannot find any rational counter-argument. Only the remnants of our souls and direct sensations tell us that not everything in Your passion for power, wealth, and war is good and that not everything in Your Trinity-Credo is true. Since it is we who have to kill and be killed in war, since it is our houses and fields that are destroyed, and our families that are ruined, since it is our bodies that painfully suffer from the excruciating wounds, and our bleached "ego" that suffers from fear for ourselves and our dear ones, these direct perceptions sharply contradict Your Credo and what it stands for. The poor remnants of our former souls suggest likewise that Your argument about Jesus and other defamers of competition are almost blasphemous, and Your formula of prosperous and decaying nations is incorrect.

The testimony of the remains of our souls and of our direct experience is reinforced by Your critics' accusations that You are one of the agencies of the Great Perverter. We cannot help responding to these poisonous innuendoes. By our psychoanalyzed ego we know that they are baseless. But by our almost defunct souls we intuit that the accusations are partly correct. This inner contradiction generates our anxiety complex. Pray, order Your psychiatrists radically to purge the remains of our souls from our bodies and egos. If need be, let them lobotomize our brains to the extent of turning us into never-worried and ever-cheerful human cows. It is better to be a contented cow than a depressed and rebellious *homo sapiens!* Long live complete psychoanalytical extermination of the atavistic soul and universal lobotomy of all little human mortals without any discrimination of sex, age, race, religion, nationality, or party!

GRATEFUL OFFERTORY TO THE IRRESISTIBLE DEITIES OF STAGE, SCREEN, RADIO, TELEVISION, AND OTHER FINE ARTS

Finally we come to You, the Beauticians of Humanity and of this Planet! We thank You for powdering our faded skin, for rouging our colorless lips, for hair-doing our bald skulls, and for perfuming our B.O. By your sex movies, sex novels, strip-tease exhibitions, hula-hula gyrations, erotic ballets, juicy descriptions of rapes and sex crimes, by "perfectly natural" sex paintings and photos, and by the sex rhythm of Your jazz bands, You successfully keep us sexually charged and ever-ready. By Your seasonal changes of Your legal mates with numerous sideline sex excursions in between, You inspire us with a marvelous example. Even the physically impotent among us feels himself an erotically drunk Dionysus enjoying the beautiful curves of Esquire's album and the clandestine Paris photos. We are thankful indeed to You for this incessant rejuvenation of our sex glands and sex organs. Keeping constantly all the varieties of sex perversion before our physical and mental eyes, You put the finishing touch upon Your sex service to us.

By Your artistic concentration upon murder You render another great service to humanity. Endless murder and detective stories, interminable murder movies, murder headlines on the front page of papers and magazines, followed by the most vivid descriptions of murder itself, murder photographed and painted, murder put to music, murder versified in poems and paeans, and especially the gigantic mass murders of wars and revolutions glorified in poetry and prose, music and painting, architecture and sculpture, movies and pageants, religious rituals and civic parades — by this artistic devotion, concentration, reproduction, glorification, and diffusion of murder You keep humanity constantly in the region of naturalistic social sewers and prevent us from the "escapist flight from reality" into the regions of sunny blue sky and spring blossoms. By all these divine operations You render to us not only artistic but great educational service. Under the influence of Your art, thousands of the youth and the grownups are successfully inspired by the murderous intoxication and learn directly this thrilling experience. This experience, especially when it is ended by the sublime *Finis* on a hangman's rope or the electric chair, insulates them — once and for all — against any escapist flight from this reality. You can be proud: thousands of these experiences can be laid at the doors of Your art.

The very fact that some 80 to 90 per cent of Your great art is centered around sex organs, police morgues, and criminals' hideouts is the most eloquent evidence of the sublimest refinement of Your art and of its ennobling influence upon us, the Freudian little bags of big libido and of strong murderous instinct.

Other marvelous details of Your Divine Art still more increase its unrivaled beauty. Instead of an illusionistic art, immortalizing mortals, You realistically mortalize the immortals. In place of beautifying the ugly, You successfully uglify the beautiful. In lieu of foolishly ennobling the ignoble, You cold-bloodedly ignoble the noblest phenomena. Instead of seeing the beautiful sun rays in a little pool of water, You see only the dirt spots of the sunlight itself. In place of the obsolescent heroic, heavenward soaring, inspiring, rejuvenating, purifying, and invigorating art of Phidias and Praxiteles, Michelangelo and Shakespeare, Bach-Mozart-Beethoven, of the art of the Parthenon and of the Gothic cathedrals, You create the most modern art of debunking, dirt-painting, enervating, demoralizing, disintegrating and drowning everything from God to man in the muck of the megalopolitan sewers. This makes Your art immortal in its unique pathology.

Bosom Comrades of Apollo and Intimates of Venus! Our

homage must be paid to another achievement of Yours. Being unable to create anything great in the old-fashioned way — in any way Your critics say — You try to re-create the masterpieces of the great creators. In past times when Andrea del Sarto, himself a notable painter, was asked to correct the position of an arm in one of Raphael's pictures, del Sarto blushingly declined the offer, saying: "If Raphael painted it so, its position is perfectly correct." When young Beethoven was invited to arrange for orchestra one of Haydn's compositions, Beethoven refused. "In order to do it right an arranger must possess a genius equal to Haydn's genius. But if he has such a genius, it is better for him to compose his own things than to distort the works of other genius. Haydn knew what he was doing; and if he wrote these things in this form, it needs no arrangement." These old-fashioned creators had an irrational respect for the achievements of other great artists. Any tampering with the works of other masters they regarded as a sacrilege.

You, Modern Music Makers, Picture Makers, Sculpture Makers, and Mass-Literature Manufacturers, You are perfectly free from these antiquated superstitions. You do not hesitate for a moment to take Beethoven or Brahms, Tchaikovsky or Bach, and make out of their masterpieces a jazz-hash or a whining mess, or the bleating love-call of a crooner. You do not have the slightest inhibition in "adapting" the male figures of Praxiteles or Michelangelo for masculine sex appeal and the female figures of Titian or Rubens for feminine seductivity in advertising trousers or swimming suits, schoolgirl-complexion soap or a rejuvenating fourteen-day-test laxative.

You feel quite free to use any religious ritual for a new strip-tease dance, a Sophocles tragedy for a Freudian burlesque, or an ancient cathedral as the stage for a comedy. As a daily routine You rewrite, rearrange, and modernize Shakespeare and Dante, Aristophanes and Lucretius, Tolstoi and Melville as You please.

In Your efficient condensation of the long and circuitous story of *Anna Karenina* or *Madame Bovary,* You turn them into fast-moving true confessions of seduced Russian or French females, with plenty of "it." *The Iliad* and *The Odyssey* are transformed into dynamic adventure tales of many gods and goddesses, Hollywood-fashioned men and women loving, kidnaping, fighting, plotting, and cheating one another. "Dynamism, brevity, efficiency, centered around murder or sex" — such is Your formula for Your marvelous modernizations.

The same formula is used by You in any condensation of any literary or philosophical or scientific or musical work. Hence the wonderful "Digest-Culture of Our Age" created by you. Thanks to You, nowadays everyone is educated — efficiently, easily, and economically — by this or that digest: Science Digest, Love-Making Digest, Gardening Digest, Religion Digest, Philosophy Digest, Fine Art Digest, Law Digest, Basketball Digest, and so on, up to the Digest of Digests and the final Digest of Digests of Digests. This ingenious Digest-Culture and Digest-Education makes even Mortimer Snerd sufficiently intelligent to take a regular part in radio programs. As for us, our whole education is obtained from the digests; our intelligence is fed by the digests; and our egos are formed by the digests. Without this invention of Yours, we would have remained complete ignoramuses!

We cannot enumerate all Your achievements. Let it suffice to say that without Your participation, no big party of the Big Immortals is thinkable; no big enterprise, private or public, can be started; and no historical event can happen. You are the unavoidable entertainers of all such parties and events.

Of course, the lunatics of the Sermon on the Mount and the old-fashioned devotees of the immortal art of the great masters (as they say) find many dark spots even on the body of Your dynamic art. They accuse You of an utter creative sterility. For this reason, they say, Your greatest and biggest best-sellers sensationally function for a few months and then are gone with the wind into oblivion forever. You can fool Yourselves and others by praising a blighter as a masterpiece, and calling a masterpiece a blighter, but You cannot fool the balance book of history: its figures are always correct. Since it writes off as waste almost all of Your creations, this sounds the death knell of Your art. It does not have any future. You try to overcome Your lack of genius by masterly techniques, an absence of quality by quantitative bigness — hence Your motto "the bigger, the better." You try to substitute a best-seller for a classic. Alas! If these subterfuges fool Your contemporaries, they cannot fool the irrevocable judgment of historical process. This judgment condemns Your art and criticism to the dumping field of history, either to be burned or to rot slowly there with other cultural rubbish.

The crazy loons accuse You further of sacrilegious distortion of the immortal masterpieces. Being unable to create anything great of Your own, You sadistically vent Your impotent sterility on the immortal art of the great masters. Sacrilegiously You distort, disfigure, and destroy it by Your "adaptations, arrangements, and modernizations." In this respect You are bigger cultural vandals than the worst of the Communists and barbarians. You sin against the Holy Creative Ghost Himself.

As a result of this sterility and vandalism, now comes Your greatest crime against the fine arts — its prostitution and its murder. In the bizarre opinion of the maniacs of the immortal art, You, Your art critics, and Your art dealers prostitute it literally by degrading art to the role of a mere stimulant of sexual activity or digestion. You degrade it by allotting to it the role of a mere bracer of jaded nerves. You debase it by making it an instrument of hate, murder and war, death and destruction in all forms. You prostitute it by turning it into a marketable commodity, a money-maker, and a mere appendix to the advertised solid soaps, laxatives, stockings, razor blades, rubber, and what not. You prostitute art by delivering it into the hands of the greedy, ignorant, and ugly art traders. You destroy it by serving through it the whims of the Mighty and the Rich and the vulgar tastes of the crowds. Your noisy critics incessantly torture it by their ignorant reviews, incompetent evaluations, and the judgments for sale to the highest bidder. Finally, You murder the immortal art each time You put it to any service of the Great Killer and Destroyer. In all of the above uses, You put it to such use.

For these reasons, the loons of the immoral art rave against You and Your art and art critics. Though their ravings do not decisively influence our balanced brains, nevertheless they somewhat affect us. The effectiveness is probably due again to the unexpurgated remains of our former soul and its delusions. Whatever the cause, we admiringly petition You, the Beauticians of Our Bodies and the Aestheticians of Our Taste, to put the finishing touches to the impeccable body of Your art and artistic activities. If for undisturbed enjoyment of Your art the remains of our souls are to be destroyed, You can do it easily in co-operation with Your psychoanalysts and psychiatrists. They have already begun to use Your art for similar purposes. Step up the process, and the task will be accomplished. Fully castrated spiritually, lobotomized mentally, with all the traces of our souls removed, we shall be completely insulated against the ravings of any lunatics of peace and of any maniacs of the immortal art.

CHAPTER THREE

Liberation and New Life

The Downfall of Big Lords and Masters

Our Lords and Masters! For half a century now we have been praying to You for preservation of our lives from the Killer and for salvation of our libidinal ego from the Perverter. Alas! Our supplications have not helped us. Either because they have not reached Your busy ears or because of Your unwillingness to relieve our sufferings — whatever the reason, our earthly lot (and Your scientists tell us we have no other) is becoming truly unbearable. Our body pains have grown beyond human endurance. Freed from the controls of ego and superego, our genital, anal, and oral libidos fight one another incessantly Our sadistic-masochistic instinct is rampant and murderously attacks the libido itself, not to mention everybody and everything it meets in its explosions. Our ego is weak and gone to pieces. Our superego is perfectly impotent. Libido, death instinct, ego, superego furiously fight one another within our bodies. Each of us is a painful mess of blind forces frantically clashing against one another. There is no peace of mind or enjoyment of body within the remains of our personality.

Meanwhile the Great Killer rapidly expands his activity. Each succeeding day he takes an ever-larger quota of our lives. Each week his taxes in our blood and suffering increase. Each night his devastation area enlarges. The Destroyer is firmly determined

67

to labor until mankind disappears from the earth and the earth itself vanishes in the space-time infinity. . . .

Our Earthly Leaders! Hard-boiled and Soft-boiled, Autocratic and Democratic, Communistic and Capitalistic, Monarchical and Republican! The time of Your leadership has run out. Our endurance is exhausted and our patience is spent. Your big promises have lost their charm. Your big checks to the banks of the future have shown themselves worthless. Our endless supplications to You have proved to be perfectly useless. In spite of the most generous use and abuse of our lives, fortunes, and labor by You, our sacrifice has been fruitless. You appear to be as dumb and unresponsive to our prayers as the clumsiest stone idols and as voracious and greedy as the big Moloch himself. Whether the reason for Your uselessness is Your helplessness in regard to the Great Killer; or Your willingness to serve him; or Your cussedness and vanity; whatever the cause You have not saved us, nor helped us, nor can You do it in the future.

In spite of the millennia of Your activities, in spite of the millions of our lives sacrificed, You have not liberated us from the Killer, or from murder, war, hatred, stupidity, ignorance, sorrow, and misery. Especially dismal has been Your failure during this century. In the twentieth century we are murdered, ravaged, decimated, plagued by all sorts of calamities more than ever before. In this century Your bankruptcy is truly complete and irreparable.

Our former Lords and Masters! Our belief in Your immortality and unerring wisdom, incorruptible justice and love for us is over. The death knell for Your leadership has just struck and is tolling mournfully. From now on our ways part asunder. You go Your way and we shall be going ours. Where Your road is leading we know not. Without any malice and grudge we wish

You Good-by and Farewell! If You want to join us as fellow companions, You are welcome!

New Man, New Earth, and New Haven

All-merciful God! We, little mortals, have parted with our former leaders and masters, former way of life and values, institutions and culture. We are abandoning our old abode and are about to enter the long and perilous road to the New Man-Creator and the New Peaceful Haven, safe from the Great Killer-Destroyer-Perverter. In this momentous hour we need more than ever before all the wisdom of serpent and all the innocence of the dove. . . .

Our first step is our prayer for all the myriads of our brothers and sisters who perished in vain in the past millennia and are still wantonly perishing at the present. *Fac eas Domine de morte transire ad vitam. Requiem aeternam dona eis Domine et lux perpetua luceat eis.* Grant them, O Supreme Soul, to pass from death to eternal life and radiant rest.

Our next prayer is for all the living who are overburdened by pain and sorrow beyond human endurance. "Ye now are sorrowful; howbeit, your heart shall be joyful, and your joy no man taketh from you." Each of us must take a share of their sorrow and must never harm anybody by thought, word, or deed. Each of us must share his joy with all the joyless and mournful. All sorrow is thus transfigured into joy and the harvest of joy is abundantly increased.

In regard to ourselves, our first task consists in the fullest restoration of our souls or our rational and superrational selves. In the era of the Great Killer, our former masters and their experts intentionally tried to exterminate our souls or selves and to turn us into libidinal-destructive bags with a sickish ego and aberrational superego. All the available means of soul destruction

were used for the purpose. They would have certainly succeeded
in this unholy task if the soul or self were mortal. The immortality of self, transcending our mortal ego (the ego of J. P.
Jones or K. S. Marshall), prevented the soul's destruction. Instead of annihilation, the soul was driven backstage and masked
by the greatly inflated sex-death instincts, lilliputian ego, and a
foggy superego.

At this point our former masters and their mind-experts tried
to turn us into soulless automata. They scientifically reduced
the total human personality to a few classes of button-units, easy
to sew into an individual, easy to cut off, and especially con-
venient to observe and to count up. In their card catalogue
they had a small card for every one of us. It contained the button-
formula of every person: so many I.Q. test buttons, so many
aptitude test buttons, so many Rorschach test buttons, and so on.
In the card's few letters and figures, each one's whole personality
was diagnosed, measured, and expressed in the precise terms of
buttons. Respectively for the mind-experts, for our former masters, and for the whole world we existed only as buttons, were
talked to only as buttons, functioned as buttons, and were treated
as buttons. After some time we ourselves began to feel increasingly like buttons, to speak as buttons, to act as buttons,
and to believe we were buttons. We almost turned into button-
automats.

Fortunately the indestructible and irrepressible self, hidden
in the buttons, prevented the complete mechanization of our
personalities. The soul finally reasserted itself, and now it is
taking supreme control of our bodies and of our minds — the
control of the bodily instincts, functions, and needs and the
mastery of mind's emotions, volitions, and ideas.

Re-enthroned as the supreme master of everyone's unconscious and conscious energies, the self now is putting an end
to anarchy and the war of instincts, egos, and superegos within

the individual and is transforming us, the degenerated human automata, into creative, harmonious, and radiant sons of God.

And what a marvelous change this reawakening of soul makes in us, in the whole of mankind, and in the whole infinite universe! With the full re-enthronement of soul, every one of us, the little human beings, becomes a possessor of the whole world. This possession makes each of us so rich that the richest millionaires of the "soulless world" are but pitiful beggars in comparison; they have only so many pieces of paper or silver or gold. We possess the infinite universe in all its inexhaustible variety of forms, lights, colors, sounds, objects, plants, creatures, movements, actions — beginning with the simple miracle of the silent opening of a flower and ending with the great mystery of creativity.

With the full reawakening of the self, each of us becomes a powerful center of creative forces inconquerable and invincible by the greatest and most buttonized army of killers, equipped with all the Satanic gadgets of destruction. None of these gadgets can kill the self while the soul can destroy the gadgets.

And what a marvel of marvels is the soul itself! When our rational ego looks at it, the ego can but wonder at the self's inexhaustible richness and its infinite creativity. Perhaps Goethe grasped something of this marvel of marvels:

The soul of man resembles water: from heaven it comes, to heaven it rises; and then returns to earth, forever alternating. It foams brightly, rolling in cloud-waves over polished rocks; then flowing with tranquillity, it softly wanders, hiding, murmuring, to the depths below it; over craigs projecting from the deep it falls, roaring, foaming, step-like, far downward. Then flowing, level, it creeps away to the meadow, and in the glassy sea gaze all the planets at their faces. Wind is to wavelet tenderest lover; wind from the deep tears foam-crested billows. Soul of man, mortal, how art thou like water. Soul of man, mortal, how art thou like wind.

With our soul reacquired, the whole world is transformed in

its appearance, meaning, and nature. The whole universe is now becoming our own home, sunny, warm, beautiful, and friendly, with no fences and trespass signs. There is plenty of room for everyone and everything and fences are superfluous. All things in this new universe are turning now into our brothers, beginning with the "Brother Sun" or "Brother Earth," and ending with "Brother Rabbit," "Brother Creature," and "Brother Man." Looked at through the eyes of the soul, the whole meaning of life and the mission of human beings on this planet are also radically transformed in this new cosmos. Life is transfigured from the soulless "struggle for existence" into the creative adventure, animated by love, helped by mutual aid, and striving to be radiantly creative. The supreme mission of humanity on this planet becomes the creative building of a great human universe of the True-Good-Beautiful Trinity. Its building is the realization of our highest nature — the nature of man, the creator, striving to ascend to ever higher and higher pinnacles of creativity.

Being the supreme, this mission is at the same time the most absorbing, thrilling, and most joyful activity of all human preoccupations. No matter whether creativity pulsates in a child's preoccupation with his toy and blocks or in a mason's arrangement of his bricks, in the invention of a new gadget or in the discovery of a new truth, in the creation of a new artistic masterpiece or of a new religious value, all creative actions — small or great — are the happiest, noblest, and the most precious experiences of a human being. More than any material wealth they enrich the creators by imperishable riches transcending millions and billions of perishable gold pieces.

The reawakening of our souls and their creative activity is already improving our way of living and enriching our life-experience a hundredfold, more than the greatest upswing of material standard of living has ever done. In this way we are solving the hitherto unsolved problems of poverty and prosperity, of miserably dull and absorbingly rich living. As a by-product even our economic plane of living is rising faster than it has ever risen before. In the past, in spite of all the whipping of the lazy slave by the master, in spite of all the coercion of the serf by the overseer, in spite of all the motives of self-interest and high personal profits, in spite of even the most scientific arrangement of the production operations in gigantic factories — these "incentives" never produced enough material values. Hard labor and sorrow, misery and discontent were our lot. Now, with the re-enthronement of our soul, its free creative impulses prove to be more efficient in production of commodities than all the rude and egoistic incentives of the past. Yea, passing by, we are rapidly solving even the never-solved economic problems.

Nay, more, much more, Brethren! The re-enthronement of our souls is already clearing the problem of death and immortality. It is rightly said: "Behold, all flesh is as the grass, and all the goodliness of man is as the flower of grass; for lo, the grass with'reth and the flower thereof decayeth." We know that the ways of flesh are mortal. We are cognizant also that the days of our ego on earth are numbered. Only the egoless soul or egoless self is imperishable, immortal, eternal, and above death. It does not have any beginning nor has it any end. It existed before any time and shall exist after any time is ended. It was not created in time but time itself was created by it. It transcends any ego, any "I," any "me" and "mine." Our bodies and egos are but temporary instruments, momentary incarnations of the immortal soul or eternal self. It is this soul that is the core of our true being. The body is born and dies. One's little ego with its selfishness and idiosyncrasies, vices and virtues, comes and goes. But the self abides forever. It is ever changing and never changes; ever moving and ever still; ever one and ever many; ever the same and ever different. It is the *coincidentia oppositorum.* It embraces in itself everything and is not identical with anything. It is all in all and nothing. It is inexpressible and indescribable by any notion, concept, word, sign, theory. Anyone who attempts to give its "scientific formula" is the greatest fool.

This renaissance of our souls inspires us with undismayed fearlessness towards the terrible Great Killer. The fully awakened self is the secret fountainhead of our unlimited courage in challenging, opposing, and eventually destroying the Unholy Destroyer. We thus rediscover what the Divine Seers of Humanity revealed long ago.

And fear not them which kill the body; but are unable to kill the soul. . . .

Know thou that that by which all is pervaded is indestructible. Of this immutable being, no one can bring about the destruction. . . . Self is unborn, eternal, permanent and primeval. He is not slain when the body is slain.

Our newly acquired soulfullness is responsible also for our strategy in the struggle with the Great Perverter and in the building of the new haven on earth. Here again we rediscover the great truths revealed long ago by the Seers of Mankind. Revealed but never followed in full, either by our former lords or by our ancestors and predecessors, these truths are simple and well known. They start with the soul's desire to have its temporary incarnation — the body and ego of every individual — as clean, beautiful, and good as possible. The self wishes it for the same reason that we desire our temporary dwelling place to be comfortable, beautiful, and good for our living there. The self does not coerce the body and ego to be good and beautiful, just as the traveler does not coerce the hotel to be radically improved overnight. But both, the self and the guest, prefer the splendid state of their temporary lodging and often suggest improvements. Sometimes they even exert some pressure upon the management. If, in spite of their suggestions the dwelling place remains hopelessly dirty, they leave it to its course of decay and move to another place.

In the free creative control of the body and ego by the soul, the self takes the loving care of both. It suggests, sometimes even commands, to the body and ego the best life-course under the existing conditions. Since the self wishes the greatest good for the body and ego, among other good things it wants that both live on this planet the maximum of their numbered days, that both realize fully the whole of their creative potential, that both enjoy the fullest and noblest happiness, and, finally, that both die the natural death when their numbered days run out.

This is one of the reasons for the ancient, universal, and perennial revelation of the Divine Seers: "Thou shalt not kill." From our rediscovery of this old truth, our uncompromising resistance to the Great Killer follows. We want the bodies of all human beings, even of all living creatures, to be beautiful and clean from bloody smears, dirty stains, ugly mutilations, and repulsive wounds. We want the egos of all human beings to be sound, creative, noble, and free from mortal sins and horrible vices. We want all "ego-bodies" to live creatively and die peacefully. Any violent death, especially the mass murders of children and innocent persons, is the ugliest crime against our soul and the universal Self. Without any exception whatsoever, no ego-body is entitled violently to terminate the life of another ego-body and to force its soul to move out before the numbered days of tenancy in these dwellings expire. Any ego-body guilty of murder of another is horribly mutilating, uglifying, and nullifying itself, not to mention the killing and mutilation of the victim. A murderer ego-body is a walking death and a rotting carcass, repulsive to its own soul, and to the ego-bodies and souls of others. The world of such murderers is the ugliest and most stenchy horror, unbearable for any self or soul. In ancient revelations such a society is called by the term of the *inferno*. It is correctly depicted as the universe of murderers and mutilators of ego-body, presided over by the Unholy Killer himself.

After our Enlightenment we are unreservedly opposed to any murder and to any harm inflicted by any ego-body upon other ego-bodies by deed, by word, and by thought. We are unconditionally committed to stop this eternal draft of the ego-bodies for a continuous repopulation of the inferno, and to destroy the inferno itself and the Unholy Killer.

But how? Would not the destruction of the inferno involve ourselves in the killing of all servants of the Destroyer, in the use of violence against and infliction of painful harm upon their ego-bodies? Would not we be forced to kill the killers and to make our own ego-bodies the murderers of other ego-bodies?

Here again the old revelations of the Seers help us to escape this eternal tragedy of the peacemakers becoming the killers in their peacemaking. These revelations do not say "Kill your enemy" and "Resist the evil by violence"; they say categorically:

Resist not evil (by violence). . . . Whosoever shall smite thee on thy right cheek, turn to him the other also. . . Love your enemy, bless them that curse you, do good to them that hate you, and pray for them which despitefully use you and persecute you. . . . Be ye therefore perfect, even as your Father which is in Heaven is perfect.

These revelations say further:

Blessed are the meek; for they shall inherit the earth.
Blessed are the merciful; for they shall obtain mercy.
Blessed are the poor in heart; for they shall see God.
Blessed are the peacemakers; for they shall be called the children of God.

These truths were revealed long, long ago, by Egyptian and Babylonian, Persian and Sumeric, Chinese and Japanese, Hindu and Greco-Roman, Jewish and Arabic Seers. Unfortunately the leaders and lords of the past, and the bulk of the led masses, have always thought that these revelations were just the fanciful dreams of abnormal lunatics — unrealistic, impractical, even suicidal. The scientific experts of the Executives and Executioners of History have again and again stated that "from the scientific standpoint, these revelations are mere nonsense, contradicting the law of the struggle for existence, the law of equality of action and counter-action, the nature of the human id and ego, and, in brief, all scientific verities."

These experts have further declared that if these rules are tried to be practiced, the result would be negative selection and the survival of the unfit at the cost of the fit, of the stupid at the cost of the intelligent, of the brutes at the cost of the kind, of the worst persons and groups at the cost of the best.

The re-enthronement of the soul in us shattered the hypnotic power of these assurances of our former lords and of their scientific experts. Since for millennia their rule of "an eye for an eye and a tooth for a tooth" has been ferociously practiced and since it has not yielded any peace and harmony for these thousands of years, we became suspicious about these assurances and started to test their "scientific validity." The very first experiments have shown that hate uniformly begets hate, murder generates murder, war gives birth to war, and no murderous crusade for any noble purpose has ever yielded or can yield peace, harmony, and creative happiness. The experiments have demonstrated further the complete validity of the revelations of the Seers. Only love and kindness can and do eliminate hate, bestiality, and murder. The only efficient method of elimination of the "man eat man" doctrine of the Great Killer and of his inferno is the Seers' method of "Love your enemy, bless them that curse you," and so on. There is no other way to eliminate the Unholy Killer, his operations and inferno. Here again the Seers have been right and the so-called scientific servants of the Perverter have been false.

Our first practices of the Seers' method have shown indeed that love is a life-giving force, necessary for physical, mental, and moral health of human ego-bodies; that altruistic persons live longer than the egoistic and especially murderous individuals and groups; that love is an indispensable condition for deep and lasting happiness; that it is goodness and freedom, beauty and justice at their loftiest which are the very heart and soul of all moral, religious and aesthetic values; that love is the most powerful antidote against criminal, morbid, and suicidal tendencies, against hate, fear, and psychoneuroses; that, together with truth and beauty, love is the only force capable of controlling freely, without any coercion, the biological and acquired propensities of man, his mentality and conduct; that its minimum is absolutely necessary for the durable existence of any society, and especially for a harmonious social order and creative progress. Finally, our practice and experiments have shown that love is the only effective force that kills the Unholy Killer and his murderous operations, by transforming the Destroyer into a Builder, the Killer into a Good Neighbor, and former murderous conduct into helpful activities for others.

Such, in brief, are the methods, strategy, techniques, and results of our non-violent fight with the Killer. They show how we are "killing" the Killer by transforming him into an unselfish friend; how we are resisting the evil without using evil means; how we are eliminating war without any bloodshed; how we act as peacemakers without turning ourselves into "crusading killers." By all this we are indebted to the divine guidance of the Seers and to the re-enthronement of the soul into our ego-bodies. This strategy permits us to build the new haven on earth without shedding a single tear of an innocent child and without taking a single life of even the Killers.

Of course, on this road to the new haven we have our own trials and tragedies. Love does not always instantaneously turn a killer into a good neighbor; neither does it always stop or prevent war. Now and then we are confronted with the greatest tragic dilemma: either wantonly to kill innocent persons or to be killed in vain among the guiltless persons. We do not accept either part of this dilemma; and thanks to the method of the Great Seers it confronts us less frequently than it does the followers of the method of the Murderous Crusades. Once in a while, however, the bitter cup confronts us. We are forced to make a choice of either to kill or be killed. In such a tragedy our soul suggests that our ego-body pray to Merciful God to be given courage to be killed rather than to kill. Now and then our ego-body cowardly fails and we succumb to the Killer's temptation. But more frequently and increasingly so, we are given this courage and our ego-bodies submit to be killed rather than to kill. In this way the sacrificial mystery of the *Agnus Dei qui tollis peccata mundi* continues to occur. Some of us become martyrs and die by the death of martyrs. But of all the fruitless deaths by violence, this martyr death proves itself as the only fruitful and marvelously creative one. The blood of martyrs seems to be the miraculous fertilizer for building the Kingdom of God on this planet. While the myriads of casualties of innumerable wars have perished in vain, without building anything of real value, the blood of less than ten thousands of Christian martyrs built the Christian world-religion and the Christian civilization of this planet. While the blood of millions of victims of civil wars, revolts, and crimes has fertilized nothing, the blood of a few great martyrs like Socrates, Jesus, St. Peter, St. Paul, Al Hallaj, or Gandhi fertilized the growth of the world's greatest values. Martyrdom triumphs thus over death itself and redeems the sins of mortals. This makes our ego-bodies quite fearless of the Killer. We increasingly become free from the Killer's intimidation by death and destruction.

Such then, after our liberation from the former masters and lords, are our ways of life and our struggle with the Killer and his forces. These ways explain practically all the specific measures we introduced after the dismissal of our former bosses. Some of these measures have been as follows:

(1) Immediate cessation of all wars, violent revolutions, "police actions" and "military expeditions" that were going on in all parts of the world at that time. When instead of our former lords and their diplomats the armistice and peace agreements were entrusted into the hands of our most sincere peacemakers, they quickly arranged the cease-fire, then armistice, then peace.

(2) Complete disarmament and complete demobilization of all armed forces in all countries; destruction of all weapons by remaking them into peaceful instrumentalities of living.

(3) Legal, moral, and religious outlawing of war, murder, and brutal violence in all forms by the World Council of Humanity and by all the states and organizations down to the family and nursery school. The outlawing is universal and unconditional. Among other things, it absolutely prohibits any government from declaring war or murderous activity of its citizens or members against anybody.

(4) Inculcation of "Thou shalt not kill" into everyone from the moment of birth. Any act of murder is now depicted as the most appalling and most horrible misfortune that can befall a human being. As a result, all of us now are simply incapable of committing murderous acts. The mere idea of murder fills us with the greatest repulsion and sacrilegious awe.

(5) Cancellation of all previous appropriations for armament, armed forces, and war of all states. Up to the last cent, the funds were reallocated for constructive purposes like the alleviation of misery, poverty, disease, ignorance, insanity, vice,

and crime wherever they occurred. This reallocation alone permitted elimination of the sharpest forms of these sufferings on
the whole planet and improvement of the standard of material
and spiritual living far beyond the highest standard that existed
at that time in the United States of America.

(6) Reassumption of a greater part of the affairs of the
former governments by the private citizens and control of these
affairs by the citizens themselves. For the management of a few
basic needs, we brought into the government the meekest, the
purest, and the most unselfish (but capable) neighbors. As a
result, the governments have increasingly become the real servants of the people, free from the corruption and cynicism, the
lust for power and the predatory habits inherent in these former
governments recruited from the most aggressive, brutal, cynical,
perfidious, and predatory politicians.

(7) Elimination and alleviation of the "man eat man" struggle for existence which at once made unnecessary the many institutions and personnel in charge of the public safety and
vested interests, the huge army of secret and open police, spies
and detectives, judges and lawyers, attorneys and politicians,
prison wardens and executioners, and other unproductive
agencies. Reallocation of the funds formerly used for these
agencies and re-entrance of their personnel into the productive
activities also helped notably to improve the standard of living.

But the main source of our progress has been the release of the
creative forces of everyone through the reawakening of soul and
a reorientation of the activities of our ego's mind. From the
moment of birth every child is now stimulated, directly and
indirectly, to develop fully his creative potentiality. The main
task of education is the utmost stimulation of the free creativity
of children, university students, and all adults.

The appropriations for constructive research and research
facilities have been tremendously increased. At the present time,

practically everyone who has a creative idea can develop and test it in laboratories and libraries equipped with all the necessary means and gadgets. As a result of this release of creative forces, discoveries, inventions, and creative achievements have increased enormously. Their increase has already contributed to the ennoblement and improvement of our lives tremendously, far beyond the boldest imagination of the dreamers of the pre-liberation period. Yea, we are rapidly solving most of the formerly unsolved problems, rapidly "killing" without killing the Unholy Killer, and rapidly building the Greatest Temple on this planet to the Greater Glory of God and the Noblest Happiness of Man. We were sorrowful. Now our heart is joyful and nobody can take our joy from us.

CHAPTER FOUR

The Law of
Polarization in Frustration and Crises

1. THE PROBLEM

What are the effects of suffering generally, and of frustration as a particular form of suffering, upon the individual's personality, integrity, creativity, and ethico-religious behavior? What are the effects of mass suffering and mass frustration in social calamities and crises upon a certain society and its ethico-religious status? What are the effects of the epochal crisis of our age upon contemporary individuals, societies, and humanity as a whole?

2. TWO PREVALENT THEORIES

Prevalent views on this matter are expressed by two diametrically opposite theories. Since almost immemorial times, one view contends that sufferings and calamities purify, spiritualize and altruistically ennoble the individuals and groups involved. Aeschylus' "it is through suffering that [moral] learning comes"; the motto of the New Testament and of other religions which states "whom the Lord loveth, He chasteneth; and scourgeth every son whom He receiveth": these are ancient formulae of this belief. John of Ruysbroeck voices it when he says that "the grace of God touches a man from without and from within. From without through sickness; or through loss of external goods, of kinsmen, and of friends; or through public disgrace. . . ." From this "prevenient grace arises a natural repentance of sins and a natural goodwill."[1] John Woolman, likewise, expresses

---

[1] John of Ruysbroeck, *Adornment of the Spiritual Marriage* (London, 1916), pp. 7-10.

this belief, saying that a smallpox epidemic and other calamities "are the messengers from the Almighty to be an assistant in the course of virtue and to incite us to consider whether we employ our time only in such things as are consistent with perfect wisdom and goodness."[2] Numerous recent examples are represented by the statements of Father Yelchaninov and A. J. Toynbee. "Our Lord has infinite pity for us, and yet He sends us suffering; it is only when we are stricken by calamity that we are able to yield a certain sacred fire. This is the meaning of wars, revolutions, sickness; I think of the meaning of sweat, tears, and blood for our purification and sanctification — of work, penance, and martyrdom. Through them the body is freed of its animal elements, and the spiritual impulse pervades the whole man."[3] Toynbee repeats this, saying that "after all, one of the deepest spiritual laws that we know is the law that 'it is through suffering that learning comes' "; that suffering is the way "for getting into closer communion with God, and becoming less unlike Him"; that "in this world we do learn by suffering."[4]

The opposite view — also very old — has been more fashionable in recent times. S. Freud, and in his wake a legion of psychologists, psychiatrists, sociologists, and moralists, maintain that suffering, calamity, and tragedy are a variety of frustration; and frustration invariably produces aggression against the direct and indirect agencies of frustration. Since aggression is possibly the sharpest form of an active egoism attacking and inflicting pain upon others, this means that suffering-frustration tends to generate aggression, enmity, and strife in all their forms, from the

---

[2] *The Journal of John Woolman* (Boston, 1909), pp. 96-97, 153.

[3] A. Yelchaninov, "Fragments of a Diary," in G. P. Fedotov, *A Treasury of Russian Spirituality* (New York, 1948), pp. 422-426.

[4] A. J. Toynbee, *Civilization on Trial* (New York, 1948), pp. 234, 248, 260, *et passim*. In justice to Toynbee it must be noted that on pp. 150-51 he vaguely mentions what I call the law of polarization; but he fails to develop it and to correct through it his one-sided view of the salutary effects of suffering, or calamities, or tragedies.

bloodiest to the mildest, from the most overt up to the hidden tendencies of animosity. Freud, viewing the search for pleasure and avoidance of pain as the primordial force of human nature, saw frustration in each instance that pleasure-seeking or pain-avoiding was thwarted. Aggression is thus "the primordial re-action" to any frustration or suffering.[5]

Frustration and Aggression by J. Dollard, N. E. Miller, L. W. Dobb, O. H. Mowrer, and R. R. Sears can serve as a conspicuous example of Freudian views among contemporary psychologists and social scientists. Trying to show themselves to be "quite scien-tific," the authors open their study with the categorical "basic postulate" that "aggression is always a consequence of frustra-

---

[5] S. Freud, "Mourning and Melancholia" in *Collected Papers* (London, 1934), Vol. IV; *A General Introduction to Psychoanalysis* (New York, 1920). In his *Beyond the Pleasure Principle* (London, 1922), however, Freud notably changed his explanation of aggression. In this work he viewed it, especially its masochistic and sadistic forms, as a manifestation of a *death* instinct — the second primary instinct, side by side with his libido. The very change of Freud's view in this matter is symptomatic of the deep fallacy of Freud's notions. He could not fail to observe that "frustration," viewed as a block to pleasure-seeking or pain-avoiding, often produces suicide, increase of internal control, unselfish sacrifice, and altruization of individuals. He tried, however, to explain all such phenomena as "aggression directed against the individual himself or self-aggression." Such a "generalization of frustration-aggression" got him into new and worse difficulties; it explicitly contradicted his "basic pleasure-seeking and pain-avoiding principle." Suicide, self-torture, self-immolation, self-control where the frustrated individual intentionally avoids many pleasures and seeks many pains are evident contradictions to Freud's basic pleasure principle. Furthermore, by extending the concept of aggression, which always means aggression against somebody or something else than the self of the aggressive person, he made his concept of aggression void of any definite meaning. The result was the complete failure of his theory of the pleasure principle and of frustration-aggression. This failure made him look for a different theory that could explain all these phenomena in a more satisfactory way. Such a theory was provided by Freud in his death instinct. This theory, in turn, is yet more fallacious than his preceding theory. It is contradicted by a legion of uncontroversial facts and irrefutably logical evidence. For this reason Freud later on practically abandoned it and left the whole matter in a messy state as concerns his theories. This footnote equally applies to a host of psychological, psychiatric, and sociological theories that blindly follow Freud and are "more Freudian than Freud himself." He, at least, saw the irremediable shortcomings of his theories, whereas these lilliputian "Freudians" do not exhibit any of the insight of their master.

tion," and that "aggression inevitably follows frustration."[6] Following this postulate, the authors deduce a series of dogmatic "generalizations" that are based (with a very few exceptions) on practically nothing but "illustrative and imaginary cases." By uncritically accepting Freud, they extend the meaning of "aggression" to "self-aggression" (self-criticism, self-control, self-suicide, self-altruization, "catharsis," etc.), thus depriving the term of any definite meaning and covering by it a series of quite different — and often opposite — phenomena.[7]

Such are the two prevalent theories concerning the egoistic or altruistic, aggressive or spiritualizing effects of calamities, miseries, sufferings, and frustration upon individuals and groups.

The very contradiction of these two hypotheses is evidence of the invalid one-sidedness of both. What serves as factual and logical evidence to support and corroborate one theory is evidence of the one-sidedness and fallacy of the other theory. In addition, a long series of experimental, semi-experimental, observational, statistical, and historical facts openly contradict the one-sided claim of either of the theories considered.

3. Four Types of Response to Frustration, Suffering, and Calamity

Contrary to the theory that suffering always ennobles, the body of evidence shows that in many cases suffering, frustra-

---

[6] J. Dollard and others, *Frustration and Aggression* (New Haven, 1939), pp. 1, 2, 27, *et passim.*

[7] *Ibid.*, pp. 46 ff. See Note 5, which applies to this blind repetition of Freudian mistakes. As a humorous detail, however, these authors find that "other conditions being constant, self-aggression should be a relatively non-preferred type of (aggressive) expression which will not occur unless other forms of expression are even more strongly inhibited." Quite a revelation! Or, here is another example of their generalization: "The occurrence of any act of aggression is assumed to reduce the instigation to aggression" (pp. 48, 50). Thus, if a bully freely bullies, his subsequent instigation to bully is reduced; if a rapist freely rapes a victim, his unhindered raping reduces the instigation of subsequent raping. It is high time that the production of this sort of nonsense, which pretentiously claims to fall in the realm of scientific generalizations, be stopped.

tion, and calamity produce not altruization — the spiritual and moral ennoblement of persons and groups — but either "dumb passivity" and stultification, or an increase of egoism, selfish aggression against persons and groups, or spiritual and moral degradation. On the other hand, the relevant factual evidence also shows that frustration does not always lead to aggressive reaction. Aggression is only one of four main reactions. In many cases, contrary to the theory of frustration-aggression, frustration in the form of calamity, misery, grief, sorrow, tragedy, or the thwarting of pleasure-seeking and pain-avoiding actions produces not an aggression against others, but three types of reactions different from aggression: (1) submissive passivity and dumb patience; (2) redoubling of the creative efforts by frustrated persons, especially creative geniuses, to transcend the frustrating obstacles; (3) searching self-criticism, self-control, decrease of selfishness, increase of altruism, religious spiritualization and moral ennoblement.

(1) It is a daily occurrence that frustrations develop in many persons and groups an unaggressive submission and dumb patience towards all the forces that block their desires and objectives.[8] Without any aggressive protest they submit to misfortunes in the same way that many of us submit to bad weather, snow, rain, drought and storms. We may suffer from this in-

---

[8] Sometimes they react intentionally in this way, for the sake of *captatio benevolentiae.* M. de Montaigne noted "that men by various ways arrive at the same end. The most usual way of appeasing the indignations of such as we have offended, when we find that we absolutely lie at their mercy, is by submission to move them to pity; and yet, bravery, constancy, and resolution [aggression], though quite contrary means, have sometimes produced the same effect." *The Essays of Michel de Montaigne* (London, 1913), vol. I, chap. 1. Edward, Prince of Wales, Scanderbeg, and Conrad III did not spare the submissives but spared the courageous and proud among the conquered, while Dionysius the Elder or Alexander the Great did the opposite. Two similar types are observed among dogs. Some try to be subservient and approach a frustrating agent with their tails between their legs; others are aggressive. Among the dogs of I. Pavlov's laboratory there were conspicuous examples of both types, respectively named by Pavlov.

clemency, but we do not shake our fists to the heavens, nor curse and attack anything or anybody. We just patiently endure and suffer. This attitude develops especially well when our first efforts to overcome the frustration prove a failure. The development of this sort of reaction to frustrations is particularly evident when a given group is conquered either by an external enemy or — in internal revolutions — by the victorious faction. At the beginning of such a conquest, part of the conquered population tries to fight the conquerors and reacts aggressively; while another part passively submits and tries to do its best under the circumstances. If the attempts of the aggressive part repeatedly fail, it also becomes "tamed," and gradually turns into a dumb-like patient, a submissive "broken reed." A tree that has been slightly bent tends to straighten but it loses this "aggressiveness to straighten" if it is broken or kept bound by a rope for a sufficiently long time. So individuals and groups lose their inclination to fight the conqueror after being broken or kept bound long enough. Some individuals and groups do not show such aggressiveness at all. It is exactly on this "passive submissiveness" that many conquerors and dictators build their domination over the subjugated populations. If, at the beginning, the dominant group must use the rudest means of coercion, punishment and terror, after a certain period of bloody tyranny, their domination becomes "natural": the population submits to the conquerors without any severe coercive measures. Slaves and serfs, outcasts and lower castes, the conquered peoples who have accepted their lot for decades and centuries through many generations without even questioning the right of their masters — these serve as solid, perennial, and universal evidence of the existence of this passive submissivity as one of the typical reactions to frustrations. History and the daily observation of the relationships between various bosses and their subordinates (frequently frustrated by the bosses) supply unlimited examples of this sort of phenomena. Some of the disabled and infirm also react in this way.[9]

(2) In other cases frustration plays the role of stimulant to an unaggressive — particularly creative — effort to overcome the frustrating obstacles by redoubled efforts that do not involve increased aggressiveness towards persons or groups. Frustration is reacted to by increased creative efforts on the part of artists, scientists, inventors, thinkers, moral and religious creators. Lord Byron's lameness forced his efforts to be a great poet. Mirabeau's ugliness made him "boil with ambition, ravenous for fame."[10] Such a catastrophic frustration as deafness did not make Beethoven more aggressive, but made him put greater effort into his creative work. The incessant frustration of poverty, the death of his mother, lack of appreciation on the part of his early patron, the Archbishop of Salzburg, up to later frustrations in his efforts to obtain the position at the Hapsburg court, failed to make Mozart aggressive, but rather stimulated his efforts to overcome all these difficulties by way of redoubling his creative activities. Many eminent scientists and technological inventors, beginning with Archimedes and ending with the Edisons, Sikorskys, Curies, and a legion of others, experienced very serious obstructions and frustrations before they succeeded in their purpose. And yet, these frustrations did not make them aggressive, but only stimulated, redoubled, and tripled their energies and efforts. Moreover, *some amount of frustration is rather necessary to stimulate the efforts and creativity of all persons,* from an ordinary individual to a genius. When things are too easy and no frustration blocks their activities, their latent

---

[9] Cf. H. von Hentig, "Physical Disability, Mental Conflict, and Social Crises," *Journal of Social Issues,* Fall 1948, pp. 21-27.

[10] G. S. Jallentyre, *The Life of Mirabeau* (New York, 1912) pp. 4-5.

energies may remain dormant or only a small fraction of their potential talent may become active.[11] Many biographers of F. Mendelssohn regret that he suffered no tragedy in his life. Tragedy, they believe, would have deepened his genius and music.

(3) Finally, in many cases, frustration and catastrophe, or suffering, is reacted to by an increase of altruism and decrease of egoism, by a religious and moral transfiguration, by the elimination or weakening of aggression, instead of its emergence or reinforcement. So many relevant, easily observable and testable facts of that sort exist that only a few typical facts need be mentioned here.

The transformation of a number of persons from self-centered and egoistic into altruistic, from irreligious or little religious into religious, from sinful into saintly individuals, is precipitated precisely through intense frustration, suffering, or calamity. The life of many a great apostle of love and modest good neighbor, of many a saint and highly spiritual leader, exhibits the role assumed by frustration-suffering-calamity as the precipitant of this anti-aggressive conversion.

The frustrations of a long illness, of being a prisoner of war, of humiliation at the hand of nobles, and of sharp conflict with his father were the precipitants of St. Francis' transformation from a golden, dissipated youth into an incarnation of the deepest, purest unbounded love.[12]

Similarly, the conversion of St. Ignatius Loyola, "up to twenty-six years of his age given to the vanities of the world," was

---

[11] From this standpoint Toynbee's analysis of "challenge and response," of a too-favorable and too-unfavorable environment in the generation of "civilizations," is additional repudiation of the criticized theory of frustration-aggression. Cf. his *A Study of History*, vol. I (Oxford, 1933).

[12] See R. Fülöp-Miller, *The Saints That Moved the World* (New York, 1945), pp. 165 ff; P. Sabatier, *Life of St. Francis of Assisi* (New York, 1927), pp. 15 ff.

started during a long sickness and painful surgical operations caused by a serious wound received in the battle of 1521. During the long convalescence he was given, along with romantic books, the *Vita Christi* and a book on the lives of the saints. In his autobiography he describes how his reverie became double: now he fancied heroic deeds and a worldly kind of love, now the kind performed by St. Francis and St. Dominic. He tells how the pleasant reveries of the first kind left him "arid and discontented," while the reveries of the second kind made him "contented and joyful." Finally, the vision of Our Lady with the infant Jesus tipped the balance and definitely started him towards his religious and moral goal.[13]

Dunstan was going to marry but, being severely sick, sent for the bishop and received monastic consecration.[14]

The first step in the transformation from a lusty sophisticated intellectual into St. Augustine was started by the *death* of his dear friend, and the last step was brought about by the *death* of his beloved mother.[15]

The Irish plague of 685 A.D. and the death of a dear companion precipitated the religious and altruistic transfiguration of Egbert.[16]

St. Teresa's transformation was precipitated by her *sickness* and fits, and especially by her most serious illness soon after her entrance into the monastery.[17]

St. Paul's conversion was precipitated by his sudden fit, blind-

---

[13] See *Autobiographie de S. Ignace de Loyola*, tr. by E. Thibaut (Bruxelles, 1924), pp. 31 ff.; H. D. Sedgwick, *Ignatius Loyola* (New York, 1923), pp. 3 ff.

[14] D. D. Knowles, *The Monastic Order in England* (Cambridge, 1940), p. 38.

[15] St. Augustine, *The Confessions* (Everyman's Library, New York, 1932), Books IV and IX.

[16] C. Creighton, *History of Epidemics in England* (Cambridge, 1891), vol. I, p. 6.

[17] St. Teresa of Jesus, *The Life, Relations, Maxims and Foundations written by the Saint* (New York, 1911), The Life of St. Theresa, chaps. IV-VI.

ness, falling from his horse and hurting himself that occurred on his way to Damascus where he was to "purge" Christians.[18] "And he fell to the earth, and heard a voice saying unto him Saul, Saul, why persecutest thou me? . . . And trembling and astonished . . . Saul arose from the earth . . . And he was three days without sight, and neither did eat nor drink." [19]

Sickness, followed by two years of solitude, marks the beginning of the conversion of Al Ghazzali, the greatest Islamic theologian and saint (b. 1058).[20]

The loss of his wife marks the beginning of Tukaram's (1608-1649) altruization.[21] The death of his beloved Fiametta, plus sickness in 1374 and other misfortunes, changed Boccaccio from a libertine and freethinker into a religious and ethical man. The shock which Raymond Lull (b. 1235) experienced when the woman he wanted to seduce reproachfully and dramatically exhibited to him her breasts, which were being eaten away by cancer, marks the radical change in his life.[22]

The death of a child played a similar role in the conversion of Jacoponi da Todi. The death of his mother was "the first and bitterest grief" in the life of Ruysbroeck, and it accelerated his piety and led him to the priesthood.[23]

The death of his wife from a snake's bite precipitated the spiritual and moral transfiguration of Chaitanya.[24]

Escape from a deadly danger played the role of precipitant for St. Tychon.[25]

---

[18] See I. Giordani, *St. Paul* (New York, 1946), pp. 8 ff.

[19] The Acts 9:4-9.

[20] See his autobiography in Field's *Wisdom of the East*. Also A. C. Underwood, *Conversion* (New York, 1925), pp. 68 ff.; W. James, *The Varieties of Religious Experience* (New York, 1935), p. 403.

[21] Underwood, *op. cit.*, pp. 55-56.

[22] *Ibid.*, chap. XI.

[23] A. Wautier D'Aygalliers, *Ruysbroeck*, quoted, pp. 68-70.

[24] P. K. Achanya, "The Renunciation and Last Days of Sri Chaitanya," *Eur-Asia*, vol. II, August 1948, pp. 589-93.

[25] Z. Gippius, *Sviatoy Tychon Sadonsky* (Paris, 1928), pp. 9-10.

The shock of his first imprisonment by the English precipitated Sri Aurobindo's conversion from an atheist and radical political fighter into a saintly yogin.[26]

A grave illness of three years' duration, culminating in a vision of the Mother of Jesus, accelerated and accentuated the saintly progress of Serafim of Sarov.[27]

A similar precipitant, namely sickness, marks the beginning of Mohammed's religious career and the conversion of St. Hildegard of Bingen. Illness and the cooling off towards her of Louis XIV caused the conversion of Madame de la Vallière, as did disease in the case of H. Cohen and F. Coppée, and the loss of his wife in the case of F. Leseur. Cardinal Newman's conversion to Catholicism was started by the condemnation of his tracts and the moral abandonment by his Protestant colleagues and friends.[28] A death sentence, commuted to long imprisonment under the harsh conditions in "the House of the Dead," changed F. Dostoevsky into an intense religious and ethical man. Deafness, followed by grave sickness (abdominal inflammation) in 1825, and other misfortunes, mark Beethoven's increasing religiosity.[29] Imprisonment precipitated the religious conversion of G. Papini. Sickness and various misfortunes were responsible for spurts of religiosity and moral ennoblement in the lives of F. I. Kinsman, Paul Bourget, Alfred de Musset, Pascal, Heinrich Heine, van Gogh, and St. John of the Cross. A bad wound received by Brother Lawrence in the Thirty Years' War, together with the horrors of the war, "kindled in him such a love of God that he could not tell whether it had increased in the more than forty years that he lived since."[30] An unlucky marriage and

---

[26] Cf. K. R. S. Iyengar, *Sri Aurobindo* (Calcutta, 1945), pp. 176 ff.

[27] Il'in, *Prepodobny Serafin Sarovsky* (Paris, 1925), pp. 20-21.

[28] See on these, Sante de Sanctis, *Religious Conversion. A Bio-Psychological Study* (London, 1927), pp. 44 ff.

[29] Cf. my *Man and Society in Calamity* (New York, 1943), p. 167.

[30] R. H. J. Steuart, *Diversity in Holiness* (New York, 1937), pp. 41 ff.

five years of "desolation" led to the almost instantaneous conversion of Catherine of Genoa.[31] Grave sickness and the danger of death turned many Renaissance libertines, like Perpaolo Boscoli, Codrus Urseus, and others, into religious and less sensual persons.[32] Eleven per cent of 3090 Christian saints, about 2 per cent of some 700 American Good Neighbors, and about 15 per cent of a studied group of Harvard and Radcliffe students were made more religious or/and more altruistic by some sort of catastrophe.[33] Moreover, a misfortune, such as being condemned to death, causes some of the recently condemned to repent, turn to God, and become more moral, while others become yet more hardened in their criminality and go to death without any repentance, cursing God and everything of moral value.[34]

A positive ethico-religious polarization (paralleled by the negative one) almost invariably occurs in a city or region, nation or other group subjected to an important calamity, whether it be war, pestilence, famine, revolution, earthquake, or flood, and so on. It is clearly exemplified by a polarization in the population of Halifax, Nova Scotia, which occurred when an explosion of two ammunition ships, on December 6, 1917, destroyed a large part of the city, killing hundreds and wounding thousands. Deeds of sublimest altruism, contrasted with actions of human "ghouls and vultures," exploded at once on a large scale.[35]

During World War II a similar polarization took place in several "thickly populated areas" which were exposed to an ammunition explosion, mass bombing, atomic bombing, or a

---

[31] Steuart, *op. cit.,* pp. 101 ff.

[32] Cf. my *Man and Society in Calamity,* pp. 165-66; J. Burckhardt, *The Civilization of the Renaissance in Italy* (London, 1898), pp. 501, 541-44.

[33] Cf. P. Sorokin, *Altruistic Love* (Boston, 1950), pp. 60, 149; P. Sorokin (editor), *Explorations in Altruistic Love and Behavior* (Boston, 1950); J. C. Penney, *Fifty Years with the Golden Rule* (New York, 1950).

[34] Cf. the facts in *Man and Society in Calamity,* pp. 164-65.

[35] Cf. many significant details of this in *Calamity,* pp. 169 ff.

calamity like the recent eruption of Vesuvius and other volcanoes in Europe and Asia. The population directly involved in the catastrophe has invariably exhibited a spectacular increase of altruism and spiritual ennoblement, side by side with a striking eruption of demoralization, human bestiality, and criminal egoism.

A systematic study of practically any and all important wars, bloody revolutions, famines, pestilences, earthquakes, floods, volcano eruptions and other forms of catastrophe clearly shows that invariably this double-faced uniformity of polarization occurs.[36]

Moreover, a systematic verification of this uniformity shows that in the histories of Ancient Egypt, Babylonia, the Greco-Roman world, China, India, and Europe almost all the important steps in their ethico-religious progress occurred precisely in periods of short or long catastrophes, or immediately after these had reached their peak. This progress was also paralleled by the demoralization and bestialization of another part of the population.[37]

To sum up: there is hardly any doubt that an intense frustration, great suffering, or a notable calamity has functioned as a precipitant for altruization of persons and groups. This effect of frustration is no less general and uniform than the effect of aggressiveness, selfishness, and animalization.

The net result of this analysis is that both theories discussed are one-sided and fallacious. *They assume that there is only one way of reacting to frustrating circumstances* (either by positive transfiguration or aggression) *whereas in fact there are several, at least four, outlined patterns of response: (a) Egoistic aggression (brutalization and demoralization); (b) dull and patient sub-*

---

[36] See *Calamity, passim,* and chaps. X, XI, XII.

[37] For the facts, see *Ibid.,* chaps. X, XI, XII *et passim.*

missiveness; (c) redoubling of creative and other (non-aggressive) efforts; and (d) spiritual and altruistic transfiguration.

4. FOUR TYPES OF REACTION TO FRUSTRATION IN THE CATASTROPHIC PERIOD: 1940-1951

All four types of reactions to frustration-suffering-calamity oc-curred on a mass scale during the period 1940-1951.[38] Millions of persons and social groups in almost all continents of this planet exhibited *an extraordinary explosion of arch-bestial and bloodiest aggression against other human beings and groups.* The twen-tieth century before the Second World War was the bloodiest of the preceding twenty-five centuries of Greco-Roman and Western history, so far as wars are concerned. It was the blood-iest and most turbulent century with respect to revolutions, civil wars, and important internal disturbances, and at least as crim-inal as any other century before.[39] The period 1940-1951 con-tinued this exceptionally bloody, merciless, and gigantic aggres-siveness of the preceding period. The Second World War, with its millions of victims, the apocalyptic destruction of almost one fifth of the inhabited territory of this planet, the numerous civil wars, endless anarchy, guerilla wars, exceptionally high crimi-nality, and demoralization: these phenomena testify that the elemental planetary explosion of aggressiveness is a response to the most frustrating, painful, and catastrophic conditions of the period. Mercy, compassion, and sympathy seem to have van-ished. Man the Killer continues to run rampant in his sadistic

---

[38] The emergence and development of these reactions for the period before 1940 in the twentieth century, and for the periods of great wars, revolutions, and other calamities during preceding centuries, are given in my *Social and Cultural Dynamics*, 4 vols., (1937-41), *Crisis of Our Age* (1941), *Man and Society in Calamity* (1943).

[39] Cf. the evidence in *Dynamics*, vol. III; and in P. Sorokin, *Society, Culture, and Personality* (1947), chaps. 31-33.

and masochistic orgy. The decade stoutly confirms that for many millions aggression naturally follows frustration, or develops hand in hand with it.

No less eloquently does the decade demonstrate the *passive submissiveness of yet more numerous millions to frustration, suffering, and calamity.* After several unsuccessful efforts to defend or regain their freedom from the dictatorial, tyrannical, or intolerable regimes of Lenin-Stalin, Hitler, Mussolini, Tito, Franco, the "democratic regimes" of Quirino, Syngman Rhee, Mao Tse-tung, and other Communist, Fascist, and Democratic Totalitarian governments, millions of revolters against such regimes, after repeated merciless suppressions, turned into "broken reeds," unable to straighten and oppose the oppressors and tyrants. They simply became "dumb human animals," patiently bearing anything their rulers imposed upon them. Moreover, after one or two decades of such passive submissiveness, they have become genuine supporters and glorifiers of their tyrannical bosses. If not the whole population, then at least a substantial part of it, in Soviet Russia or China, Indonesia or North Korea, in the Third Reich or Italy, in Spain or in several Latin American countries, has changed from being bitter opponents of the regime to loyal and enthusiastic followers of their oppressors. The total number of these people has to be computed by tens, perhaps even by hundreds of millions on this planet. The decade strikingly corroborates that passive submissiveness (which sometimes turns into loyal adherence) is an unquestionable reaction to frustration, as common and frequent as the reaction of aggression.

The transcendence of frustration by a creative effort is universally and always a much less frequent response than aggressive or submissive reactions. Creativity is a very rare flower in comparison with the weeds of aggression and submissiveness. It becomes especially rare in periods like ours, when a hitherto existing dominant (sensate) form of sociocultural order disintegrates and a new form is only at its inception.[40] Nevertheless, a few of these rare flowers have blossomed as a reaction of creative geniuses to the decade's frustrations. A number of scientists made important discoveries in the mathematical, physicochemical, and biological sciences. Atomic discoveries were only a part of these. A number of inventors and engineers created and constructed atomic plants, atomic bombs, new types of airplanes, and many other gadgets. Several biologists discovered new medical preparations. Unfortunately, a large part of the discoveries and inventions in the physical and biological fields turned out to be destructive and deadly, rather than constructive and vitalizing. In this respect they were one of the important manifestations of the aggressiveness of the period. Nevertheless, a part of these discoveries and inventions was peacefully constructive. It served the needs of life and not of death; it was motivated by altruistic love, and not by hatred; and it facilitated the forces of harmony, co-operation, and good will, instead of the forces of hate, death, and destruction. Insofar, this part of the discoveries and inventions was a manifestation of a creative response to a frustrating calamity.

The same is true of the decade's creativity in the fields of religion, philosophy, ethics, law, social sciences, humanities, and the fine arts. Though the total creativity in these fields was relatively insignificant; though a large part of revived beliefs, philosophies, theories, ideologies, and art creations was negative rather than positive, hate-laden rather than love-laden, demoralizing rather than integrating, debilitating rather than revitalizing, dragging into the muck of social sewers, rather than lifting *per aspera ad astra* — nevertheless, a small portion of these creations was mentally, morally, and aesthetically ennobling and socializ-

---

[40] See my *Dynamics* and *Crisis of Our Age*.

ing, and inspired the love of God, the world, and one's fellow men. Insofar, their authors transcended the endless frustrations of the period by creative effort.

Finally, the decade also witnessed a notable upsurge of altruistic love, compassion, empathy, unselfish sacrifice, ascetic stoicism, revived spirituality, and revitalized religiosity. An altruistic and spiritual response to the decade's endless frustrations also emerged and grew, side by side with the other three responses. A few of these reactions have been mentioned above and others will be mentioned further on, when the decade's forms of polarization are discussed. For the present these brief indications are sufficient to show that all four types of reactions to frustration-suffering-calamity were evidenced on a mass scale during the decade discussed.

This means that all the other variations of the one-sided theories of "frustration-aggression" or "frustration-altruistic spiritualization" are one-sided as, for instance, the theory that claims the invariable increase (or decrease) of criminality in periods of crisis and catastrophes, or the theory that asserts there is an invariable increase of religiosity (or atheism), spiritualization (or demoralization), creative renaissance (or creative decay) in periods of calamities. Each of these one-sided theories sees only one effect of frustration-suffering-calamity instead of the above four effects, and especially the polarized effects of increased aggression and altruistic love, demoralization and moral ennoblement, spiritualized religiosity and sensual atheism, dumb submissiveness and dynamic creativity.

Having indicated this, we can now leave the responses of submissive passivity and creativity and examine more closely the forms of individual, social, and cultural polarization which took place during this period.

5. THE LAW OF POLARIZATION IN FRUSTRATION, CRISES, AND CALAMITIES

This basic law or psychosocial uniformity is still unknown to the public at large, as well as to social scientists and psychologists. Defined, analyzed, and demonstrated elsewhere,[41] it can here be formulated in a still more generalized form than in its earlier delineation. In this generalized form the law of polarization states that *a crisis, calamity, or frustration tends to make explicit and open the implicit and hidden contradictions, whether in one's mind and conduct, or in a social group and institution, or in a given culture.*

A. Polarization in an Individual. If there is a covert split in the mind or overt conduct of a person, under the conditions of calamity or crisis it becomes overt. The polarization assumes one of the following three forms: (a) If the contradictory tendencies are about equal in strength, then the mind and conduct of a person remain split into two irreconcilable parts that war with each other, the one denying what the other affirms, the one destroying what the other constructs. The individual becomes a split personality. (b) If there are several multilateral contradictory tendencies, the individual's mind and behavior disintegrate, becoming devoid of unity and consistency. Both turn out to be "jerky," confused, incoherent, and abnormal. (c) If the contradictory tendencies in the individual are unequal in strength, then the strongest tendency overcomes the weaker ones. As a result the individual now becomes much more consistent and intense in his dominant (strongest) tendency or trait. If, for instance, in contradictory tendencies of "sinfulness and saintliness" the sinful bent happens to be stronger, such a person, during a crisis or calamity, becomes much more intense and

---

[41] Cf. P. Sorokin, *Man and Society in Calamity*, chaps. 9-12.

consistent in his sinfulness than before the crisis. If the saintly bent in him is potentially stronger, then under conditions of some tragedy, he becomes much more saintly than before. The same is true of any contradictory tendencies in the thought, words, deeds, or relationships of an individual. Polarization in a person expresses itself either in the appearance of an open and un-abridgeable split in the mind and actions (when the contradictory bents are about equal in strength), or in a neurotic disintegration of his personality (when there are several or multilateral con-tradictions), or in an intensification of the strongest contra-dictory tendency, elimination of its opponents, and a correspond-ing broad or fanatical integration of the person.

B. *Polarization in a Group or Institution.* Under the con-dition of calamity a covert and potential contradiction among the members of a group becomes overt and actual; it grows in its intensity and splits the group into openly opposed factions. Its extreme poles tend to grow at the cost of its central, balanced majority. For instance, under normal conditions the majority of a social group is neither particularly saintly, nor particularly sinful. It tries to render unto God what is God's and unto Caesar what is Caesar's. Under conditions of calamity this majority begins to melt from both ends: a part of its previously balanced members becomes more sinful, while another part becomes more saintly than before the crisis. The group thus becomes polarized, and an open conflict flares up between its opposed factions.

Under normal conditions the political majority of a group is made up of the totality of balanced, moderate parties. The extremely reactionary or revolutionary parties are almost always a minority. When a severe catastrophe befalls the group, its political split becomes more drastic; its extreme parties tend to grow at the expense of its moderate parties. Political conflict becomes intenser and more violent. The group polarizes politically.

A similar polarization in a group may occur in connection with many other contradictory values and interests, if and when these are important for a given group at a given moment. Religious, economic, artistic, political, philosophic, ethical, juridical, and other contradictory values and interests cause the polarization of many social groups. In a great calamity the group polarization tends to become "multilateral" or "total," involving many sets of contradictory values and interests and splitting the group into two or more irreconcilable factions warring ruthlessly with one another.

C. *Polarization in a Culture.* Under the conditions of catastrophes a hitherto hidden contradiction between meaningful cultural values or phenomena becomes explicit. Becoming open, the contradiction leads to an open fight for survival or domination of the contradictory values. In this struggle sometimes the weaker value, defeated by the stronger, disintegrates, whereas the stronger value grows in integration and power; sometimes both competitors mutually destroy each other, giving a victory to a *tertius gaudens,* to a third value that either transcends both fighting values, or synthesizes their positive merits, or just happens to be favored by lucky circumstances. In both cases the defeated cultural values disintegrate, become increasingly incoherent, and lose their prestige and influence.

The polarization in cultural values is paralleled concretely by an enormous intensification of the struggle between the partisans (individuals and groups) of each competing value. The competing values appear to their partisans as the end values, as the absolutes that do not permit any reconciliation, any compromise. As a result the struggle itself often turns into a bloody strife in which each party tries to destroy its opponent *ad majorem gloriam* of its cultural value. The struggle for the domination and existence of various religious values, with their religious wars and bloody suppression of heretics; the struggle of various political values of monarchies or republics, with their civil wars and revolutions; the fight between Capitalism and Communism, regimented and free enterprise, democracy and despotism, with corresponding "cold" and "hot" wars: these are examples of this sort of cultural polarization.

Such, in brief, is the central point of the law of polarization and its personal, social, and cultural forms. We can now turn to a generalized summary of the main personal, social, and cultural changes brought about as a result of the crisis' coming of age during the period 1940-1951.

6. POLARIZATION IN THE MIND AND BEHAVIOR OF THE SENSATE INDIVIDUAL, 1940-1951

During the period under discussion (1940-1951) the polarization in the Western sensate person has enormously developed in all its main forms: (a) as a sharp cleavage in the soul and conduct of a person; (b) as a disintegration of the sensate mind and conduct, resulting in an increase of "confused" individuals and of mental diseases, especially various psychoneuroses; (c) as a reintegration around opposing sets of values, resulting in an increase of extreme and mutually opposite types of persons with a consequent intense struggle between them. Let us glance more closely at each of these forms.

A. Split in the Soul, Personality, and Conduct of Western Sensate Man. The Nazi, the Fascist, the Communist, the atheistic, even the democratic and officially religious sensate persons afford striking examples of split souls, split minds, and split personalities on a large scale, typical of the overwhelming majority of the Western population. Not the whole soul and conduct of a Nazi, or a Fascist, or a Communist is black, beastly, selfish, cruel, cynical, or inhuman. Such is only one part of their soul and behavior. The other part is conspicuously unselfish, compassionate, human, ethically and socially noble. Side by side with the unspeakable cruelty and inhumanity manifested in the coldblooded extermination of millions of their enemies, in bestial actions perpetrated against millions of innocent victims, the Nazis, Communists, and Fascists have displayed a supreme devotion to their cause which far transcends the egoistic interests of each member of these parties. Unhesitatingly they have sacrificed for their cause many personal advantages, profits, comforts, and even their lives. If anything, in their readiness to sacrifice themselves for their cause they have been more altruistic, more generous, and more ethical than many a bourgeois or Babbitt, or a pharisaic preacher of Christian love and unselfishness.

In the same Nazi, Communist, or Fascist we have two entirely different egos, minds, souls, and forms of conduct. One is supremely beastly, the other is truly human. One is highly egoistic, the other conspicuously altruistic; one is destructive, the other constructive; one is materialistic and hedonistic, the other notably idealistic, ascetic, and stoic. One is a pitiless killer; the other is willing to be killed for an idea or for the well-being of the Third Reich, the Communist Fatherland, the proletarian dictatorship, or the corporate state. Thus we have Dr. Jekyll and Mr. Hyde in one and the same person. This sharp dualism has also been demonstrated by many war veterans of democratic countries.

In a milder form a similar split has occurred in millions of democratic and officially religious individuals. On the one hand they have maintained their truly democratic or Christian mind and conduct. On the other, they have professed ideas, set forth standards, and performed deeds quite contradictory to their democratic or Christian ideas, standards, and actions. Their right hand declares complete liberty of religion; their left hand starts a violent crusade against godless Communism, heathen Nazism, Japanese Shintoism, or "perverted and subversive heresies," punishing their adherents with all available punishments. Their right hand condemns government regimentation of business, nationalization, and socialization. Their left hand incessantly calls for government interference in business and labor-management relationships, for government nationalization and control of industry and now, as in war time, of practically the whole economic life of the country. If a Communist government regiments business, such a democratic person considers it bad, "a suppression of free enterprise." If Roosevelt, or Truman, or Attlee, or even de Gaulle does the same, it is declared to be democratic, wholesome, and conducive to prosperity and free enterprise. If Communists suppress liberty of speech, it is bad; if democracies suppress it in regard to their "subversive" opponents, it is "freedom of speech and press." If the Communist government tries to obtain a small portion of Iranian oil, the action is branded as "unmitigated aggression." If democratic countries grab practically all the oil of the Americas, of Africa, of the Indies, of the Middle East, including Iran, this is declared to constitute democratic, unselfish help to the backward countries. If the Nazis violate international agreements, it is "a crime against humanity and God." If the democracies violate them by wholesale strategic bombing, even by the use of atom bombs, this is called a perfectly legitimate means of warfare. If the North Koreans kill American prisoners of war or South Koreans, it is called "inhuman atrocity"; if American phosphorous, jellied gasoline, and other bombs inflict most torturous death upon tens of thousands of the noncombatant Koreans, or if the South Koreans torture and kill North Koreans, it is either glorified unashamedly or is passed by as something normal and not atrocious at all. If the Nazis turn Jews into D.P.'s it is "an unmitigated evil"; if the Zionists turn a million

Arabs into D.P.'s, it is considered a much lesser evil, even something justifiable. If the Soviets "liberate" a country, it is branded as "tyrannical aggression"; if democracies bring death and destruction to millions in Korea, it is called "Christian and democratic liberation."

The right hand of the democratic countries "doesn't want an inch of territory that does not belong to us." Their left hand unhesitatingly grabs the whole Pacific Ocean and turns it into an inner United States lake, with all its islands and other possessions; extends (under the form of the Monroe Doctrine, or the Marshall Plan, or some other name) its sphere of influence over practically the whole world except the "recalcitrant and aggressive Soviet bloc"; creates its own puppet governments, displays all the signs of highhanded aggressive imperialism; and remains seemingly undisturbed by this glaring contradiction! In other democracies the repudiation of territorial expansion expresses itself in Italian and German colonies' mysteriously falling under British control. Their humanitarianism protests against the executions of a few political leaders by the Soviet bloc governments, while they engineer and condone the executions of thousands by their Greek, Turkish, Korean, Iranian, or Japanese puppet governments. If a Soviet villain commits these actions it is extremely bad; if a democratic person perpetrates them, this is extremely good. If the Soviets arrest one hundred or a thousand of their enemies, it is outrageous. If the Dutch or the French engage in war against millions of their colonial population, it is condoned and now and then even represented as humanitarian assistance to a backward people. Now the majority of the United Nations enacts the universal bill of rights and prohibits genocide unconditionally. Now the same majority sanctions and condones atomic and bacteriological warfare, saturated bombing of cities and villages, destruction of the means of subsistence of millions of "enemies," and other forms of a gigantic genocide and of an absolute denial of all rights of millions of persons.

This sort of split in the soul and conduct of a democratic sensate person has become so common and so habitual that we often fail even to perceive it or to understand its pathology. Sometimes we label it "hypocrisy," "bigotry," "elastic diplomacy," or the like. But even these terms do not adequately describe all the depth of the split. In a slightly different form it represents the same split which has occurred in the soul and conduct of the Nazi, Fascist, and Communist sensate person.

Thus we live and act in a universe of split minds and personalities. The Western man of today has largely a dual personality, like that of Dr. Jekyll and Mr. Hyde. This is the first form of abnormal polarization experienced by Western man on a mass scale. These split personalities are to be counted by tens of millions; 99.99 per cent of them are outside mental institutions, and they are to be found in the upper, the middle, and the lowest social strata. Their percentage is likely to be especially high among the upper governmental leaders, the business and labor aristocracy, the administrative hierarchy of large religious organizations, and leaders in many professions, including science, education, the fine arts, and technology. *Split personality in this sense is the first form of mental disease in the case of the Western sensate person of our time, and especially Western sensate leaders.* Its world-wide epidemics are a result and a sign of the growth of the crisis during the past twenty years.

B. Disintegration and Confusion of the Mind and Behavior of the Western Sensate Person. This form of polarization in an individual manifests itself, first, in the notable increase of functional mental disorders or psychoneuroses during this decade. Officially we are told that one of every ten individuals in the United States is bound to have some form of functional mental trouble and be in need of a psychiatrist or become a patient in a mental institution. The period has been a veritable heyday for all sorts of psychiatrists, psychoanalysts, clinical psychologists, mental healers and quacks. Never before has there been such an enormous demand for all kinds of mental doctors. Beginning with the nursery school and kindergarten and ending with the colleges and universities, monasteries, and prisons, almost all institutions have been hiring psychiatrists as necessary members of their regular staff. One seems to think that without a psychiatrist nobody can be sane, get along well, and be "adjusted." Psychiatrists and psychologistes, replacing the old-fashioned guardian angel, are now regarded as necessary for everyone, from idiots to geniuses.

Never before have there been so many courses in abnormal and clinical psychology, in Freudian and other brands of psychoanalysis, in psychosomatic and other forms of psychiatry. Courses on our inner conflicts and mental problems have been offered at universities, high schools, even divinity schools, as well as centers of adult education. Never before has the press — newspapers, magazines, and all sorts of periodicals, highbrow and lowbrow — given so much space to these problems. The same is true of radio and television, the cinema and stage. Never before has the book market been flooded by so many best-sellers on these topics and disciplines. Even in his most optimistic moments Freud hardly ever dreamed of his works' becoming such universal best-sellers. The success of books on abnormal, clinical, psychoanalytical, and "screwball" psychologies has been so great that it has seduced many a clergyman to write books on "peace of mind" or "peace of the ego" or "peace of self," in which they unhesitatingly make congenial companions and bedfellows of Jesus and Freud, identifying the libido and id with God's grace and charisma, or God with the superego, and so on. And what is still more symptomatic is that a host of Christian ministers and leaders swallow these atrocious concoctions and increasingly prescribe them to their parishioners and patients.

All these phenomena unquestionably demonstrate that the Western world has become a sort of lunatic asylum, in charge of thousands of mental healers of all sorts. Mental abnormality tends to become Western sensate man's normal state; the lunatic asylum his normal home; some sort of psychiatrist his guardian angel.

Those who escape the polarization of split souls and personalities are caught in the polarization of officially certified mental disorders.

Those who escape both these forms of personality disintegration fall into other forms of mental, moral, and behavioral confusion (polarization). Like the above-described split souls, these other forms of mental disintegration are not officially called "mental disorders," and are not treated in mental institutions. Nevertheless, they are as much a form of mental confusion as the officially recognized functional disorders of the mind. A large portion of the Western population has been exposed to so many diverse and often contradictory ideas, beliefs, standards, patterns, and values that it has increasingly become unable to digest them and integrate them into any sort of system or unity. As a result these diverse and contradictory materials lurk in the mind of this population, and the mind itself has become a sort of dumping place, without unity, consistency, or order. What was integrated before is now disintegrated; what new elements are introduced, remain largely unintegrated. The result is utter confusion, inconsistency, and instability of the mental, moral, and behavioral activities of this part of the population. It has become a rudderless boat, a prey to all sorts of windy leaders, of mental and moral epidemics, of delusions and witch hunts, of hateful emotional currents, and especially of fear in its various forms.

In this confused state this collective mind increasingly sees plots, spies, and enemies at each corner; it is worried, jittery, and afraid of various sociocultural "spooks"; it is more and more unable to distinguish true from apparent reality; friend from an enemy; a true value from a false one, a sound leader from a blind one; it increasingly loses its peace of mind, its contact with, and grasp and appreciation of, true reality; it increasingly lives in a world of phantasms and illusions. As a result its adjustments to reality increasingly fail. Conflicts pile, creativity declines, maladjustments multiply, sufferings increase, and life becomes more and more unhappy, empty, and meaningless. Such is this form of mental and behavioral disintegration. Not formally registered as a mental disorder, it is nevertheless as grave a disequilibrium of mind as the official functional disorders.

C. *Reintegration and Polarization of Intolerant Fanatics.* The last form of polarization in the individual consists of a fanatical and desperate reintegration of sensate and relative values into some sort of absolute values. A part of the sensate population has succeeded in reintegrating its sensate values around this or that central sensate interest, particularly lust for power and prestige, lust for wealth and material comfort, and lust for sensual pleasures. Ideological reintegration around these values has assumed very different forms: Communist, socialist, democratic, Fascist, Nazi. There is even a pseudo-religious variety of the struggle for power on the part of various Christian and non-Christian political mechanisms.

As these sensate values and interests are scarce, as the demand for power, prestige, fame, popularity, material comfort, wealth, kisses, copulation, and other sensual pleasures far exceed the possible supply, the individuals and groups, each fighting for a maximum share of these values, cannot help coming into collision with one another. The conflict requires that each faction shall consciously or unconsciously regard its specific ideological brand as something absolute (contrary to the relative nature of all sensate values), as the only brand entitled to exist and unconditionally dominate over all the competing factions and their ideological values. These other factions and values are declared to be unbearable, an incompatible evil, something that must be uprooted by all means, including physical extermination of the opponents and competitors. In this way several sensate systems of values are deified by their supporters. These turn into narrow-minded fanatics; mutual intolerance flares up to unprecedented heights, amidst a hypocritical profession of tolerance, and results in a series of great and small, bloody and "cold" wars of sensate factions with one another followed by wars between sensate factions and those who hold integralist (ideational and idealistic) values.

The bloody struggles of monarchists with republicans, of Nazis and Fascists with Communists, socialists, and democratic liberals, of Communists with all non-Communists, of socialists with Communists and non-socialists, of democracies with all groups who have a non-democratic way of life; the extremely cruel persecution of all non-Communists by the Communists; the incessant crusades for the extermination of Communists and the nations that support them by various anti-Communists and diverse denominations in the name of Christ and God; the "cold" wars waged by the denominational factions of the Christian nations amongst themselves and against non-Christian religions and atheists; the conflicts between the partisans of capitalism or free enterprise and the socialists, laborites, nationalizers, and Communists; the now "cold," now bloody, combats between labor and management, employers and employees, between different factions of labor unions (with their jurisdictional disputes), between the public at large and this or that union or firm, between the government and the opposition, between different unions, occupations, classes, regions, and political parties — these have become a normal trait of the period. Finally, the Second World War and numerous wars between Hindustan and Pakistan, Jews and Arabs, North Korea and the United Nations, colonial-master nations and subjugated colonial peoples, the gigantic civil wars in China, and the smaller wars in Greece, the Dutch Indies, Indo-China, Persia, and dozens of other countries — all these conflicts are likewise typical.

Peace and order have disappeared through continuous small wars and through world wars and revolutions. In each of these the fighting factions have not hesitated to declare themselves to be the chosen and the infallible, and all their opponents to be damned and deserving of extermination. Each faction crusades against its opponents with a ferocity far greater than that of the Roman government against the Christians, the Mohammedans against the Christians and vice versa, the Catholics against the Protestants and heretics and vice versa (in the period of the Reformation and the religious wars). Each elevates its often lilliputian values to a sort of absolute deity and declares different values irreconcilable and heretical. Amid the hypocritical hymns to tolerance, broad-mindedness, and freedom of belief and thought, a cynical fanaticism and an intense intolerance have grown to fantastic levels rarely witnessed in human history. Nowadays it seems that everybody is crusading against everybody, and without compunction is ready to destroy the opponents. Besides millions of small crusades, the vast blocs of nations and the vast religious organizations are busy making "Atlantic," "Pacific," "Christian," "Communist," "Jewish," "Democratic," "European," "Asiatic," "Mohammedan," and other pacts or crusades on a world-wide scale against their real or imagined opponents — crusades in which all the destructive means of warfare are to be used to their maximal limits. The polarization of intolerant fanatics has reached its maximum. The number of veterans who have gone insane, like the Camden killer, is only one of many manifestations of this sort of polarization.

Such is the third main form of polarization of individuals.

All three main forms considered — the split of the soul and personality of the individual, disintegration and confusion of the individual's mind and conduct, and the fanatical reintegration of the limited and relative values with sensate cynicism, lust, and intolerance — sum up the principal types of destructive polarization in individuals during the last decade.

D. *Constructive Polarization and Reintegration.* Fortunately the polarization of an individual has not been limited to these destructive forms. Side by side with these, the decade has also witnessed the beginning and slow growth of a creative reintegration of mind, conduct, and the whole personality. This has centered around the supreme integralist (idealistic or ideational) value systems. These systems naturally transcend all sensate systems of reality or value. Besides the purely relative nature of sensate values, the very disintegration of sensate values, their struggle with one another, the destruction, bloodshed, and misery which the recent civil wars of various sensate values and their factions with one another have wrought — all this makes a creative reintegration and positive polarization around these values impossible. Any such attempt would only add one more sensate faction in this civil war of numerous sensate cliques with one another. For a truly creative reintegration one has to go far beyond sensate values, into the realm of integralist value systems.

These integral systems view the true reality or value as a manifold infinity with sensory, rational, and supersensory-superrational aspects. The sensate aspects and values are real; but they are not the only aspect and values, and are hardly paramount. These new integral systems give a legitimate place in their value systems to the greatest and noblest sensate values, but they do not make them exclusive. Viewing them as relative, and viewing human beings as incarnations of sensate, rational, and suprasensate and suprarational forms of value or reality, these reintegrated systems categorically refuse to sacrifice human beings to any idolized sensate value; to justify any war for any sensate value; to idolize any sensate value as an end value, sufficient to justify the murder of thousands or millions. Being relative and conditional, all true sensate values can be made compatible and reconcilable according to these integral systems. Those which are negative or empty values can be eliminated by non-violent forms of resistance. Sensate capitalism and Communism, sensate totalitarianism and democracy, even sensate atheism and pseudo-religiosity (a political machine masked by religious screens) can coexist without the extermination of opponents or the destruction of the lives and values of millions of innocent people.

Since the true reality or value is manifold infinity, it manifests itself in infinitely varied forms, none of which can claim to be a full and absolutely adequate manifestation of this infinity, with all the others being regarded as false. But each of the true manifestations can claim to be a genuine, finite, and limited realization of the Infinite Manifold. Thus Christianity is certainly a genuine manifestation of the Infinite in this empirical world; so also are Taoism and Confucianism, Judaism and Hinduism, Buddhism and Mohammedanism, even agnosticism and atheism. One can be proud of his Christianity and at the same time can tolerate, even genuinely admire, these other religions without any sense of contradiction, religious sin, or moral compromise. On the other hand, the very nature of the Manifold Infinity prohibits anyone from considering himself as a monopolistic possessor of all the truth and nothing but the truth, and from regarding all others as damned or erring or irretrievably wrong. All such persons and groups sacrilegiously put themselves in the place of God and elevate their finite nature to the position of the Manifold Infinity. Such religiosity is but utter irreligiosity. It is, in reality, merely sensate lust for power and for monopolistic domination. It is a most egoistic claim to be chosen by God, with all the others condemned to hell. Being sensate lust for power and privilege, such sensate pseudo-religions naturally cause intolerance, strife, and war. The new integral systems, on the contrary, represent tolerance and admiration of values different from their own as an intimate, organic part of their own. Through these multicolored and multipatterned forms of manifestations of the infinite, the whole of humanity becomes richer, happier, and more creative in its values and possessions.

This, then, is the main direction of this constructive reintegration and polarization. It is still a minor stream, but this minority is growing from day to day. Gandhi, Albert Schweitzer, the American Friends (or Quakers), the conscientious objectors, many a genuine pacifist, thousands of small sects and groups trying to realize in their deeds the principles of the Sermon on the Mount, or of the Bhagavad Gita or the Dhammapada, or just the Ten Commandments (freed from their tribal limitations), and millions of anonymous "good neighbors" who daily perform the deeds of true love and co-operation — these are examples of persons and groups that demonstrate this reintegration.

In a very diluted, impure, and superficial form, but on a much vaster scale, this stream is represented by a part of the "Moral Rearmament Movement," by the Conference of Christians and Jews, by the United Nations, by many organizations for "One World," by vast institutionalized religions, by members of certain political parties and governments, by various labor unions, and the like. Unfortunately, however, despite their noble declara-

tions and preachings, these vast organizations still remain predominantly sensate and tribal in their actual deeds and political
activities.

Such, in brief is this positive polarization and reintegration.

7.   INTRAGROUP AND INTERGROUP POLARIZATION

The decade also witnessed an intragroup split and polarization of the members of the group in an enormous number of
social organizations and the intergroup polarization of a multitude of social groups into extreme and opposed alliances or
camps.

A. Intragroup Polarization. An enormous number of groups,
internally peaceful and united in normal times, during the
calamitous decade in question split into two or more antagonistic
factions. These opposite factions have grown at the cost of the
balanced central body of membership. The internal peace and
unity of such groups has been broken, and a "cold" or bloody
intragroup civil war has replaced the previous solidarity of the
members. This intragroup polarization has occurred not only
in political groups and organizations, but in practically all kinds
of organized groups and institutions, including the family, the
Supreme Court of the United States, and business, occupational, and religious organizations. The members of millions of
families are split into followers and opponents of Communism
or Nazism or Fascism or the New Deal, pacifism, atheism, or
Catholicism, and so on. In millions of cases the split is so sharp
that children have denounced their parents to the authorities,
or vice versa; brothers and sisters have turned into bitter enemies;
and hateful discord has replaced the unity of the family. In
millions of families the discord has manifested itself also in a
growing intolerance and incompatibility of husband and wife
and has led to a vast increase in desertion and divorce.

In religious groups the intragroup polarization shows itself in a split of many denominations and sects into two or more factions. The Russian Orthodox Church is split into bitterly antagonistic factions of supporters and opponents of the Communist government; German and Italian and largely European Protestant and Catholic organizations have been split into the allies or enemies of the Nazi and Fascist regimes and into the supporters of pro-Communist and pro-Western regimes. Among the Protestants the split has also manifested itself in the continued increase of various Protestant sects and denominations. Similar splits have occurred in the Anglican Episcopal Church, with the "Red Dean" and a minority supporting the Soviets, and the majority opposed to them.

The split is much deeper than appears on the surface. It is often masked by a "hush-hush" policy. Beginning with such a small conflict as that of a few professors of Boston College with the high Catholic authorities about the impossibility of being saved outside the Catholic Church and ending with hundreds of other problems pondered by millions of believers and answered in opposite ways, the polarization is going on within many religious organizations and in millions of souls.

An attempt is being made to counter it by the establishment of various "interfaith," mainly Catholic, Protestant, or Jewish organizations; of several "world councils of the churches"; of Protestant "world conferences" and similar efforts to reintegrate and consolidate religious organizations. These efforts are hopeful and are likely to grow in the future. For the present, however, they do not compensate for the process of splitting and discordant polarization going on in the religious bodies.

Still more conspicuous is the split within *occupational, business, labor, trade-union, and other organizations.* Their members are polarized into left-wingers and right-wingers. In many cases the polarization leads to an open split of the group into two or more different organizations; in other cases it turns the group into a house divided against itself, still united externally, but internally torn apart into mutually fighting and hating factions.

As to the *political organizations,* their internal split and polarization is truly striking and often bloody. The members of practically all political parties are split into irreconcilable factions, bitterly opposed to each other. In Communist, Nazi, and Fascist parties an intraparty split has led to a series of bloody purges and exterminations of one faction by another. In democratic and republican, liberal, socialist, labor, farmer, progressive and center parties, it resulted in a split of each party into right-wingers, left-wingers, "Dixiecrats," and the like, each wing acting independently, each excluding its opponents from the party, each assailing and discrediting the opposite faction. Even in the United States the united Republican or Democratic party has practically ceased to exist. Each is openly split into two or more parts or even independent parties. Still more striking is the intrapolitical party polarization in countries that have undergone a severe catastrophe.

The members of presumably the most impartial political institutions, such as the Supreme Court of the United States, have shown this polarization by rendering an extraordinarily high percentage of split decisions (such as five versus four) during the decade considered. This means that the decreased unanimity and increased discordance in the field of ideas, convictions, opinions, beliefs, and evaluations have led to a similar decline of unanimity and an increase of disagreement among even the nine justices of our highest court.

It goes without saying that the split and polarization among the lower courts and among the legislative and executive branches of the state governments have increased still more. The same is true of *the body of citizens of practically all states and empires.* In many states this has manifested itself in a series of bloody civil wars of the citizens with one another. In other states it has led to a "cold war," interrupted now and then by some local bloody clashes of one body of citizens with another. In all such states the polarization shows itself in a *deep cleavage of the citizens into the partisans of the existing government and into enemies that intensely hate it and are hated and persecuted by the government*. The ordinarily neutral majority of citizens tends to be replaced by the opposite factions which hate each other. The unity and peace of the states are replaced by strife and antagonistic polarization.

The same may be said of practically all sorts of social groups, organizations, and institutions. They have all been split and torn apart by the opposite polarization of their members.

B. Intergroup Polarization. Side by side with the intragroup split, intergroup polarization has enormously increased during the decade. Many groups (or their factions) have banded together into larger, sometimes very vast, alliances and thus confront one another as bitter, often implacable opponents. Although this intergroup polarization has aligned itself along different multilateral fronts, all these numerous fronts have tended to converge and to be consolidated into two or three main fronts of intergroup polarization. In each intergroup polarization the balanced, moderate, central groups have tended to give way to extreme, opposite groups. These eventually have become the poles around which the intergroup split and polarization have proceeded, resulting in the emergence of two inimical camps, each made up of several consolidated groups.

Polarization of *political parties* is manifested in a decrease of the votes for the moderate parties of the center and in an increase of votes for the polar extreme parties. Most of the moderate parties of the center have decreased in membership, some even disappearing from the scene. On the other hand, most of the votes and parties have consolidated around the extreme political parties, Communist and conservative. They constitute two irreconcilable camps hating and fighting each other. The polarization is already world-wide and results in world-wide political strife.

Polarization of the *states* has become world-wide too, and has split all the states into two camps led by the United States and the Soviet Union. Though objectively both camps have many traits in common, and though their mutual interests demand their co-operation, yet the logic of the crisis has made them enemies. Though any new global war would be suicidal to both camps and though their "cold war" undermines them both, yet both camps openly muster their military forces, prepare all the apocalyptic means of mutual destruction, and are seemingly ready to murder tens of millions of innocent persons.

Whatever may be the real virtues and merits of each camp — and each has some of these — in this suicidal polarization the virtues of both camps are largely annulled and their vices are cultivated. As a result the anti-totalitarian Atlantic Pact is already infected with many vices of Communist or Fascist totalitarianism, whereas the Soviet bloc is hopelessly contaminated by the extreme unconcern and callousness ascribed by Communists to feudal and capitalist masters toward the life, welfare, happiness and dignity of their "subjects," the majority of the population. The leaders of both camps seem to be quite willing to sacrifice millions of their subjects for purposes which remain vague even to the bosses of each camp. Their highfalutin phrases are hardly believed even by the bosses themselves. The insanity of this polarization makes its elemental nature — the result of sensate disintegration — particularly clear.

A minority has opposed this suicidal polarization and demands instead the co-operation of both camps. A large section of humanity voices this objective through mere preaching or speech reactions; only a small minority tries to realize it through overt conduct. Eventually, however, this minority is likely to grow into a real majority, disgusted with the inept, selfish, and destructive policies of the leaders of the American-Soviet strife and polarization.

Similarly, the world is sharply polarized, in regard to the *economic regime,* into clear-cut partisans of Communist-Statist-Totalitarian-Nationalized-Socialized economy, managed mainly or exclusively by the government, and into the followers of free enterprise or capitalist or privately managed economy. Each camp increasingly becomes intolerant toward the other. Their struggle leads not only to a continuous "cold war," but now and then to bloodshed and great loss of life. The voices of individuals and groups trying to reconcile both systems, viewing them as merely relative values incapable of justifying any war and sacrifice of human life, are increasing; but such voices are still in the minority. This form of polarization is still mainly an antagonism between two sensate factions, each viewing its economic regime as the end value, as the most powerful determiner of historical processes, and each sacrificing millions of innocent victims to the idol of either Communist or capitalist economy.

Intergroup polarization in the field of *religion* shows itself in an increasing tension in a "cold" or bloody war between the partisans of a militant atheism or religious indifferentism and those of especially militant, well-organized, dogmatically orthodox religious denominations. Here also, as in the field of political parties, moderate, liberal, balanced religious denominations tend to lose their membership and leadership, and extreme atheists and fundamentalists tend to become the leaders of a world-wide religious split and polarization. Around these opposite poles, other religious or anti-religious groups federate and band together. Indifferent or atheistic Communism and Roman Catholicism are now the poles around which the religious intergroup polarization takes place. These opposite and extreme denominations have engaged in mortal combat, without any mercy and quarter for one another. The rest of the religious and non-religious persons, groups, and denominations have aligned themselves along either Communist or Catholic fronts.

Only a small minority has so far remained outside and above these two camps. For this minority the struggle of Communism and Catholicism is a fight of two political machines rather than a struggle between true religion and atheism. True religion is tolerant toward all other religions, including even atheism; true atheism is also tolerant and indifferent toward all beliefs and philosophies. The fanatical intolerance of both sides, their mutual persecutions, coercions, and even bloody strife, are the traits of intolerant political machines rather than of true religion or true atheism. The Sermon on the Mount prohibits Christians to use any coercive, punitive, physical pressure and any Machiavellian means, even in regard to an enemy. It prescribes only one policy — that of inexhaustible love for all. From this standpoint some of the anti-Communist policies of various religious crusaders are, in the opinion of this minority, not religious and Christian, but purely sensate political activities, little different from those of a Communist camp.

This line of polarization is still secondary in comparison with the main Communist-Catholic cleavage, but this minority line is increasing and may turn out to be the main line in the future.

Intergroup polarization in the field of *ethics, morals, and law* manifests itself in several forms. First, there is an increase of *open and reckless sinners,* the advocates of "wine, women and song," criminals, cynical politicians and partisans of "kill and rob" in order not to be killed and robbed, on the one hand; on the other, in an increase of the *more saintly and more unselfish* persons and groups at the cost of the neither too sinful nor too saintly majority of normal times. Both extreme factions have increased, while the solid and balanced majority has decreased. Second, there is *a decrease of the influence of all balanced and moderate ethical and legal ideologies in favor of extreme ideologies of vulgar hedonism and primitive utilitarianism on the one hand, and of stoic and ascetic ethics of love and duty on the other.* Truly Epicurean hedonism (which is very stoical) and the utilitarianism of Bentham and John Stuart Mill are replaced now by the vulgar "pleasure principle" of Freud and company, or by the precepts of Kinsey's "sexual behavior," or by the utterly primitive utilitarianism of our statesmen and politicians who have not hesitated to use atomic bombs or wholesale strategic bombing and have openly advocated the use of the most destructive means available against all enemies and opponents. These Communists and anti-Communist blind pseudo-utilitarians staged the trials of war criminals for acts perpetrated in other forms by the victorious judges themselves, "liberated" innocent Korea by bringing death to millions of Koreans and by destroying the whole country in the name of Communism and Democracy. This utter bigotry, primitive and shortsighted utilitarianism and hedonism (hypocritically covered by Christian highfalutin phraseology) would have horrified the Greco-Roman and Victorian utilitarians and hedonists. They would have been dumbfounded by the degeneracy of this sort of dominant morality of the West and of their utilitarian and hedonistic ethics. In this respect the ideologies and behavior of our Western crusaders against unmoral and godless Communism are hardly better than the morals, mores, and laws of the Communists, which are at least free from the hypocrisy of misusing the Christian principles of the Sermon on the Mount for covering their bestialities.

Side by side with the rise of this stupid utilitarianism and primitive hedonism we witness also a rise (though only in its initial stage) of the *uncompromising ethics of love and unselfishness, a Stoic asceticism, or true Christian or Hindu or Con-*

fucian-Taoist or Mohammedan or Buddhist ethics and morals. Beginning with Gandhi and his co-workers, Albert Schweitzer and his circle, the Quakers, as well as many ordinary "good neighbors" among Christians and non-Christians, persons and groups have appeared that increasingly practice these universal and perennial ethics. Though still in a minority (but daily increasing), they are deeply saddened by the prevalent hypocrisy, by the contradiction between what the majority preaches and what it practices, by the scientifically and ethically invalid prevalent moral ideologies, by the abundant cynicism and demoralization, and their destructive consequences. Being dissatisfied with all this, they turn to the eternal principles of love and unselfishness formulated in the Bhagavad-Gita, the Dhammapada, the Bible, the Koran, or in other great religious and ethical sources. They try to practice fully these principles, and by their example they inspire others to follow them. As a reaction to the prevalent carnal hedonism and stupid utilitarianism they become more and more ascetic, stoic, and "Spartan." As a reaction against atomized and relativized ethical values, they stress more and more the universal and unconditional nature of ethical values. Finally, instead of stressing rights, they increasingly stress duty. Instead of glorifying the struggle for existence, the benefits of competition and rivalry, the ethos of success and victory over one's competitors, they follow the principles of co-operation and mutual aid, of sacrifice and humility, of reverence, benevolence, and love toward all.

This is still a small minority current, but it is likely to become the main stream in the future constructive period of human history. Neither the remnants of the previous majority of moral Babbits, nor the utterly demoralized, disintegrated sensate fanatics, nor the physically and spiritually debilitated crowd of primitive hedonists and utilitarians can serve as a moral foundation for a new creative order of humanity. Only this minority can accomplish the task.

A similar intergroup polarization has occurred in virtually all fields of intergroup relationships. As we shall see in the next section, it did not even pass by scientific, philosophical, artistic, and other groups and organizations. They are also split into various alliances, for X and against X. Unfortunately they do not limit their disagreement to purely ideological differences, but reinforce it with various pressures, and with "cold" and even "hot" wars. In Soviet countries all scientific, philosophical, artistic, moral, jural, and other theories that diverge from the dominant ones approved by the government are suppressed, and their authors and followers are arrested, banished, or executed. In the anti-Soviet countries the same split and suppression take place, in a milder form so far, in regard to all pro-Soviet theories and ideas, and their "subversive" authors. "Subversive" scientists, philosophers, artists, educators, doctors, engineers, and other professionals are prohibited from teaching, from government employment and public service, and so forth; their books and publications are entered on an *index librorum prohibitorum;* some of these are confiscated and prohibited from being placed in libraries; some of the authors are imprisoned, banished, or, contrary to the letter and the spirit of the law, deprived of their citizenship and deported. In brief, intellectual groups and persons of all sorts are split into consolidated bands of two inimical camps warring with each other just as mercilessly as other antagonistic camps.

To sum up: *mankind and its numerous groups have tended to form vast intergroup alliances polarized around the extreme wings of each camp.* The intergroup polarization has taken place along thousands of "fronts." These numerous splits and polarizations have tended, however, to consolidate *along two main fronts.* One — up to this moment the most important — is *a consolidation into vast inimical camps of various sensate groups and individuals.* The other is increasing estrangement between all sensate groups and a growing minority of integralistic, ideal-istic, and ideational groups.

The main front of the internecine civil war of various sensate groups with one another has been shifting and will continue to do so. In the period 1939-1945 the main polarization of sensate groups and persons occurred along the line *pro-Nazi-Fascist and anti-Nazi-Fascist.* Thousands of groups — states, political parties, trade unions, occupational, economic, religious and cultural groups, scientific, philosophical, artistic, ethical, and juridical or-ganizations — all consolidated into these two unholy camps and launched the murderous Second World War.

In spite of millions of victims, the destruction of one fifth of the inhabited territory of this planet, the infinite sorrow and suffering, the disintegrating sensate world evidently could not quench its thirst for hate and power even by means of this apocalyptic war. In its mental and moral insanity it simply can-not live without rivalry, hate, murder, and destruction. Even before the armistice was signed, a new main front of inter-sensate group polarization emerged with its hatred, "cold war," and fever-ish preparations for a Third World War. This front now has become *pro-Soviet-Communist and anti-Soviet-Communist.* In the post-armistice years, thousands of social organizations, politi-cal and economic groups, including the states and religious, scien-tific, philosophical, artistic, and other professional associations, again split into these two camps with corresponding hate, plots, "cold war," and bloodshed. As in the first pro-Nazi and anti-Nazi consolidations, the polarized and mutually hating Soviet and anti-Soviet camps use all the unholy means, all the dishonest tricks whereby they can injure each other. In addition they openly prepare to launch a new super-apocalyptic war! In committing suicide, the insane sensate world threatens to destroy mankind itself.

If this war is launched, and if anything of this planet is left after it is over, one may be sure that even after the Third World War, amid the wreckage of humanity these demented sensate groups will not live in peace. They will again consolidate into two mutually hating camps along some new main front and, if still dominant, will release a new war. Such is their destiny at the stage of disintegration of sensate culture and groups.

The shifting character of the consolidated sensate groups may also lead to a replacement of the present-day *Communist and anti-Communist* line by quite different main fronts, such as *Asia vs. Europe, East vs. West, colonial vs. master nations, universal religion vs. universal atheism, the Anglo-Saxons vs. the Slavic or Latin world, world federation vs. national sovereign states, world federation vs. world centralized and autocratic government, totalitarianism vs. laissez-faire or free society, the poor vs. the rich, strict monogamy vs. free love,* and what not.

The hatreds and friendships of mentally and morally unbalanced patients shift rapidly. The same is true of the disintegrating sensate groups. However, the second half of the decade considered is marked by these pro-Soviet-Communist vs. anti-Soviet-Communist camps as the main line of intergroup polarization of sensate organizations and persons. This front is now dominant.

Much less noticeably, without any spectacular battles, the polarization of groups and persons is proceeding silently along the line *sensate vs. integralistic, idealistic, and ideational.* Though still in a small minority, an ever-increasing number of persons and groups have alienated themselves from all Soviet and anti-Soviet sensate factions, sensate pseudo-values, and sensate politics. In different terms, with different theories, ideologies, and beliefs, these persons and groups consider all the disintegrated sensate values and methods hopeless, devoid of true creativity, incapable of leading man out of world catastrophe into a peaceful and creative era. Practically all sensate factions and parties appear to them devoid of wisdom, blinded by lusts and passions, utterly selfish, greedy, cynical, hypocritical, and demoralized, leading not to an earthly paradise, but to an inferno. Likewise, present-day sensate culture and values are considered by these anti-sensate groups and persons as degenerate, empty, often vicious pseudo-values. They would not regret the peaceful passing of the sensate world. The attitude of these anti-sensate groups and persons is akin to that of the early Christians in regard to the sensate Greco-Roman world. They want to stay *au-dessus de la mêlée*, abstaining from the fratricidal murder of various sensate factions and groups. They include many small, "queer," and highly refined religious sects and groups, the conscientious objectors, peacemakers, partisans of non-violent resistance to war, the Quakers, ethical and religious pacifists, thousands of various unselfish, altruistic persons and groups, an ever-increasing number of integralistic (idealistic and ideational) ideologists, artists, educators, even a few statesmen and business leaders.

While various factions of the sensate world are mutually destroying one another, this minority is a sort of *tertius gaudens*, preparing for the leadership of humanity when the sensate camps have wrought their mutual destruction. Various groups and individuals of this non-sensate minority are increasingly consolidating into one camp through their negative attitude toward sensate groups and through rapidly progressing disintegration of sensate culture and values. In addition, like any growing minority, they have the vigor, the energy, the spirit, the heroism, the enthusiasm, the unselfishness, and the creativity necessary for future leaders. A minority now, it will be the leader tomorrow.

8. POLARIZATION IN WESTERN CULTURE

In the main compartments of Western culture the polarization manifested itself during the decade considered in three main forms: (a) sensate science and arts, philosophy and pseudo-religion, ethics and law, politics and economics, and the whole sensate way of life continued to disintegrate, becoming either uncreative, or vulgar, or destructive, or all three. Various sensate forms increasingly clashed and fought ferociously with one another, thus speeding their disintegration. (b) The eclectic efforts to overcome this sterility by mixing sensate with integralistic (idealistic or ideational) elements increased, but most of these efforts have been about as fruitless as ever. (c) The first signs of the emergence of integralistic (ideational and idealistic) sciences and arts, philosophies and religions, ethics and law, politics and economics, appeared at a pole opposite the sensate pole. Though this stream is still very weak (quantitatively and qualitatively), the polarization of the whole of Western culture between the poles of declining sensate and emerging integralist is growing.

A. Further Disintegration of Sensate Culture. In *sensate fine arts* the decade has not created anything of note. Even in the field of architecture it has merely continued, without improvement, the creative *élan* of the previous decades. One can hardly find any truly great sensate painting, sculpture, musical composition, or even literary achievement. At best, a few works are either good imitations or variations of the great sensate art of the preceding period. Others are atrocious distortions and repulsive vulgarizations of the magnificent creations of sensate art of earlier centuries. Not only are we incapable of creating great things, but we have even lost our reverence for them: we distort and disfigure, vulgarize and profane them without even realizing our sacrilegious offense against the creative spirit. On a mass scale our band leaders and popular composers jazz and rape Beethoven and Bach, Tchaikovsky and Liszt, Wagner and Chopin, the great operas and oratorios, the spirituals and noble religious music of past centuries. Similarly, in our "digest culture" we abbreviate, condense, and digest for the reading public the great literary compositions of the past, reducing *Anna Karenina* or *Madame Bovary* to a lurid sex story of a Russian or a French female, with their seductive males. In our modernization of Shakespeare, we have made out of his tragedies something atrociously "Hollywoodish" and "Mainstreetish." For the rest, the bulk of our best-sellers, written to an increasing extent by women (a trait typical of declining sensate culture), is the lowest grade of imitative sensate pseudo-art, ranging from *The Egg and Some More Eggs* and the Freudianized King Solomon or Henry the Eighth, to more highbrow but still more hollow volumes. The very transience of these best-sellers which, within six months, are gone with the wind, testifies to their vacuity and worthlessness. They represent business for various book clubs and other manufacturers of intellectual chewing gum, but they have not the remotest relationship to real creativity. The same is true of all the highbrow literary guides, art critics, and art-advisers. In reality they are but commercial agents of the book business. Of these vacuous writings nothing can survive for even a few years. Like a newspaper or magazine, they are forgotten as soon as they are published.

These sterile conditions explain, and partly even excuse, the open drive of the Nazi, the Soviet, and several other governments and religious bodies to encourage an honest imitation of classic art and to discourage a continuation of this hopelessly sterile pseudo-art. Imitativeness has always been a typical characteristic of sensate art during its decline. This governmentally advocated imitativeness of the classic patterns, so similar to Augustan and subsequent imitative phases of Roman art, is only what is to be expected.

In the field of *sensate philosophy, religion, humanities and social sciences* similar decadent characteristics have prevailed. A multitude of feeble imitators and lilliputian vulgarizers have replaced the eminent sensate creators of the earlier period and the much smaller but still notable figures of the end of the nineteenth and of the beginning of the twenties centuries. We have had hundreds of little Marxians and Freudians, instead of Marx and Freud; hundreds of thousands of little Communists instead of Lenin, Trotsky, or even Stalin; thousands of petty positivists, empiricists, semanticists, operational methodologists, pragmatists, natural philosophers, phenomenologists, existentialists, scientific historians, sociologists, anthropologists, economists, and so on, instead of Comte and Spencer, Durkheim and Weber, Pareto and Tarde, Mommsen and F. de Coulange, Rostovtzeff and Murray, Husserl and Whitehead, James and Royce, Henri Poincaré and Mach, E. Taylor or F. Boas, Marshall and Simiand. No figure comparable in stature even to Mary Baker Eddy has emerged in the field of religion. The decade has been pitifully barren as far as sensate creativity in these fields is concerned. This sterility would be still more conspicuous if one were to survey the works and authors who have been declared to be the most outstanding of the decade. The so-called "Semantic" distortion and vulgarization of the works of hundreds of eminent thinkers, Oriental and Occidental, who some two thousand years ago said all the sound things that are in this semantics, and said them incomparably better — this Semantics has been declared to be the epoch-making last word in science and philosophy and scientific thought.

A few books on the sexual behavior of males or females have been another "epoch-making" contribution of the decade to its biosocial sensate trash. By many "authorities" they have been placed on a par with the greatest works in the biological and social sciences. The naïveté of this sensate advertising is now perfectly clear, and these works, like hundreds of similar works before, are already largely forgotten.

In a similar way, partly naive, partly ignorant, and partly commercial advertising, dozens of books dealing with various psychological tests and psychiatric tests, testing nobody knows what, dozens of boring statistical monographs often devoid of elementary logic and serious thought, have been proclaimed as epoch-making contributions to their respective fields. While their real contribution to knowledge has been negligible, they have been considerable contributions to the bankbooks of their publishers and authors.

The very drive itself, boasting and sensationally declaring an insignificant thing to be a great value, is an indication of the desperate desire of sterile sensate culture to create something great. Alas, so far history has refused to grant this boon! And it is doubtful whether it will grant it in the near future.

In the field of *natural sciences and technological inventions* the decade disproved one of my statements, but corroborated the main statements concerning the science and technology of our age. Since my conclusions about the movement of scientific discoveries and inventions were made on the basis of data ending in 1908, these statements were accurate and valid. Subsequent discoveries and inventions from 1908 to the present time, however, have shown a rapid upward trend after the declining trend of the end of the nineteenth and the beginning of the twentieth century, especially in the fields of the mathematical, physico-chemical, and technological engineering disciplines. Whether we measure the trend by the number of discoveries and inventions or by their importance, the mathematical, physicochemical, technological, and partly even biological sciences have experienced a real revival and upswing.

However, my main statement about the making of more and more destructive discoveries and inventions, which will undermine sensate culture and finally the natural sciences and technology themselves — this statement has been decisively corroborated. Morally and socially irresponsible sensate science and technology have developed numerous destructive forces, such as superbombers and the atomic bomb; they have unrestrictedly applied these inventions to the human world, including universities, laboratories, and other seats of science and technology; they have killed millions of human beings and have ruined about one fifth of the inhabited area of this planet, including many universities, laboratories, libraries and machines. Sensate science and technology continues to concentrate increasingly on the invention of destructive methods in order to use them in the next international or civil war. These means promise to be apocalyptically destructive and constitute the greatest menace to humanity, its life and culture, and to science and technology themselves. In this way these boons of humanity have turned into the greatest destructive forces. So long as they remain sensately indifferent to moral and social duties, they are the most powerful forces tending to destroy the sensate world.

Finally, in the field of *ethics and law* the decade demonstrated the utter degeneration of purely sensate moral values. Having been relativized before so as to abolish the difference between right and wrong, the lawful and the unlawful, during the decade in question this utter demoralization demonstrated itself pragmatically and operationally in the form of the Second World War, in which all moral restraints were removed and all laws, human and divine, were violated by virtually all the parties involved. Similar nihilistic consequences occurred in the multi-

tude of revolts and civil wars of the decade, in which the opposing parties treated each other in the most bestial manner,
committing cold-blooded crimes and unspeakable atrocities on
a mass scale. In general the moral decadence of persons and
groups in their private and public behavior has been enormous.
The decade harvested what had been sown by the preceding
decades of suicidal sensate ethics and law. Millions of human
beings paid for this demoralization with their life, happiness,
dignity, and material wealth. Under the cover of highfalutin
"liberation from aggression" etc., all the parties spread death and
destruction over their opponents and innocent neutrals. Without
hesitation they accepted the motto: "Strike first and kill millions
of innocent persons in order not to be killed yourself among the
innocent millions." It is needless to add that the decade did
not witness any even remotely masterful formulation of a utilitarian, or hedonistic, or even nihilistic, system of sensate ethics
and law. What has been uttered by various sensate puppets in
this field have been merely childish, fatuous, and vulgar reitera-
tions of previous masterful formulations of sensate ethics. Even
the Freudian pleasure principle is a crude reiteration of utilitarian
and hedonistic principles expounded by Epicurus, Lucretius,
Bentham, and Mill. Sensate ethics of the decade has been a
still cruder reiteration of the crude Freudian, Jungian, Adlerian,
and similar utilitarian or hedonistic pseudo-ethics.

The sensate culture of the epoch has created a sort of ethical
creative vacuum. Our culture has tried desperately to fill this
vacuum by any available means. First of all, it has sought to
create a moral hero that could fill the vacuum. "An office boy
becoming president of a big corporation," Babe Ruth or some
other football-baseball-screwball hero, military leaders, successful
politicians, finally even Gandhi and Schweitzer, all have been
used to fill the vacuum. It of course remains as vast and empty
as ever.

Such has been the negative, disintegrating polarization of sensate culture in the decade considered. It has gone from bad to worse in its suicidal madness. This disintegration is one of its poles. The opposite pole is the new synthesis of integralistic or idealistic or ideational culture. But before passing to it we shall pause to consider the intermediary eclectic attempts to create a new culture, predominantly sensate, but intermingled with idealistic and ideational elements.

B. The Eclectic Efforts to Reintegrate Our Culture. Most of the creative efforts of the decade assumed the eclectic form of re-creating decaying sensate culture by mixing its elements and forms with those of the ideational and idealistic. Most so-called "modernistic" efforts of the decade in various fields of Western culture fall under this head. Most of them, unfortunately, have turned out to be either unsuccessful or at best moderately successful. The bulk has remained an eclectic mixture devoid of creative unity; others have displayed mastery of technique not matched by the inner content of the *opus*.

Most of the compositions of Stravinsky, Shostakovich, Prokofiev, Hindemith, Harris, Hansen, Poulenc, R. V. Williams, B. Britten, Béla Bartók, and other leading composers of the decade belong to this eclectic class. Some of their works are openly programmatic, and their program is of mixed sensate, idealistic, and ideational character, whether it be Stravinsky's *Mass,* Schuman's *Ode,* Shostakovich's *Leningrad Symphony,* Bernstein's *Jeremiah Symphony,* or Britten's *Peter Grimes.*

The same may be said of the bulk of most important modernistic paintings and sculptures of the decade: cubistic, pointillistic, dadaistic, expressionistic, symbolistic, surrealistic, intuitive, and the best impressionistic and Gothic revivals. Very few of these have succeeded in achieving a creative unity of form or content, or have gone beyond an imitation of older patterns.

The architecture of the decade has constituted mainly a wholesale war destruction of great architectural buildings of the past, a spread of the ugliest chicken coops (Quonset huts and the like) of wartime construction. Even the bulk of postwar building activity remains on the low level of supplying the needs for cheap, utilitarian housing in which the purely aesthetic needs play a very modest role. A few bigger structures, like that of the United Nations, remain, according to Frank Lloyd Wright's opinion, on an eclectic, functional-utilitarian level. The world is still looking for the truly great architectural creations of the integralist type.

The significant literary works of the decade, such as plays like *The Death of a Salesman,* or the "Existentialist" plays of Camus and Sartre, or *The Iceman Cometh,* or the satirical-political plays of the Soviet stage (of Simonov and others), and novels and poetry of the type of T. S. Eliot, Sinclair Lewis' *Godseeker,* Pearl Buck's Chinese stories, T. Wilder's *The Ides of March,* the novels of Aldous Huxley, *The Razor's Edge* by Somerset Maugham, *The Days and Nights* by Simonov, the works of Caldwell, Hemingway, Steinbeck, Faulkner, Waugh, and so on — these all, by means of their explicit content, reflect the complete disillusionment and repudiation of sensate culture and its values and look (not very successfully) for a non-sensate type of culture and values. Among all the significant literary works of the decade there appeared hardly a single work that remained hopeful of, and faithful to, sensate values and culture.

Into the same eclectic class fall most of the important achievements in the field of *philosophy, religion, humanities, social sciences, ethics, and law.* The short-lived success of Existentialism, with its eclectic mixture of Descartes, Kierkegaard, Nietzsche, Dostoevski, and what not; revivals of Neo-Thomism, mixing Thomist scholasticism with modern science, of Oriental and Occidental Mysticism (the Yoga, the Vedanta, the Bhagavad-

Gita, Ramakrishna-Aurobindo movements, the revival of Pseudo-Dionysius, Erigena, Master Eckhardt, Böhme, St. John of the Cross, etc.) by people like Dean Inge, Rufus Jones, the Friends, Aldous Huxley, and many others; revivals of Neo-Neo-Platonism, and of various forms of idealism and "phenomenologism" — these mark the decade. In spite of the official support of materialistic philosophies by the Soviet government, not a single notable materialistic philosophy has emerged. What has emerged is a pitiful reiteration of great materialistic systems of the past. Various philosophies of pragmatism, instrumentalism, operationalism, positivism, and empiricism likewise have not produced anything spectacular; if anything, some of their representatives have moved nearer to a sort of idealistic philosophy.

The strictly sensate works in the social sciences and humanities which imitate the natural sciences and claim to be rigidly scientific have barely discovered anything new or even temporarily impressive. Innumerable monographs filled with the most fanciful psychological, and psychiatric tests, which soon turn out to be testing nobody knows what; statistico-sociological and anthropological works packed with formidable tables, formulas, indexes, photographs, and terms; and an enormous quantity of "scientific" works generously financed by the government and the foundations, especially during the war: either these have been stillborn, or have rapidly fallen into oblivion after creating a little stir among the devotees of this or that pseudo-scientific cult.

Finally, the most important statutes or legal documents of the decade — the Atlantic Charter, the Constitution of the United Nations, the Declaration of the Inalienable Rights of Man, even the unfortunately used Declaration of Crimes against Humanity — all these law norms have been eclectic in character. Their sensate elements have been generously intermingled with idealistic values, without any organic unity.

Even in *science and technology* this eclectic movement has assumed notable proportions. An overwhelming majority of scientists and inventors eagerly participated in the discovery, invention, or improvement of atomic bombs and other means of destruction. They did it conscientiously, because they well knew for what these means were being prepared. Most of them have even been proud that they took part in inventing the atomic bomb, and many have sanctioned its use in Japan. On the other hand, terrified by the prospects of the general use of the atomic bomb in future wars, they have vociferously warned humanity of the tremendous danger, have advocated some sort of international control, and have then continued to participate in the improvement of the destructive power of all these means of warfare. Their right hand does what their left hand refuses to do!

In this respect their behavior is very similar to that of many religious leaders and politicians. They also vociferously pray to God for peace, and indefatigably reiterate their abhorrence of war, militarism, armament, and bullets instead of bread. In their actual behavior, however, even in democratic countries, they stand for the almost unlimited militarization of the world; for spending hundreds of billions for military purposes; for the unlimited expansion of the armament industry and for the export of arms to all the allied countries; for an unlimited propaganda of hatred toward their opponents; for crusades against all who dare to disagree with them, and so on. The post-armistice years have been not years of peace, but years of unprecedented militarization of the Soviet Union, the United States and, through these two nations, the rest of the world. One could hardly invent a more self-contradictory moral eclecticism!

C. *Emerging Idealistic-Ideational Reintegration.* The gain

of the integralist, idealistic and ideational movements for the period considered has consisted mainly in a growing paralysis of sensate culture, and especially in the growth of eclectic efforts toward cultural reintegration. As shown, these eclectic efforts in all compartments of culture have liberally introduced integralist, idealistic and ideational values for the rejuvenation of sensate values. By means of this liberal infusion of elements of idealistic and ideational culture these eclectic movements have undermined the domination of the sensate forms, proclaimed their bankruptcy, and thus paved the way for the future growth of an integralistic, idealistic or ideational culture in pure and creative forms.

The decade rendered almost universal the idea that no patching up of sensate culture can terminate the catastrophic chaos and sterility; that for its own salvation and a creative renaissance mankind has to look beyond any form of sensate culture toward new idealistic or ideational cultures. The decade decisively alienated from the sensate culture millions of human beings and shifted their allegiance to integralist values. In its suicidal self-destruction sensate culture has lost its main attractions: material comfort, material prosperity, material security, pleasure and utility, prevailing over pain and disunity. The sensate culture of the decade destroyed all security, killing tens of millions, destroying material comfort, prosperity, health, happiness, and pleasure for a large part of humanity. Thus the sensate culture lost its very *raison d'être*.

Millions of people openly but blindly revolt against a particularly oppressive variety of sensate culture, and land in the swamp of another form of it. Rebels against capitalist sensate society land in a swamp of sensate Communism; rebels against sensate Communism land amidst various no less sensate crusaders against Communism; and so on.

Other millions pack their ships with sensate, as well as with idealistic and ideational, values and depart from the sensate shore in the hope of arriving at a new land where they can build a magnificent home of integralist culture. Unfortunately most of these get lost in the ocean fog and rarely reach their port of destination. They spend their lives on a sea of eclectic efforts.

Some of the rebels, however, achieve some form of integralist or idealistic or ideational integration. They do this in two different ways. The majority do it by simply taking over, without any drastic modification, one of the great idealistic or ideational systems of the past. Christians appropriate one of the Christian denominations, with all its dogmas, ritual, and hierarchy; Mohammedans or Hindus do the equivalent of this. Some of these even enter monasteries and become monks, ascetics, priests, or hermits. In the last few years their number has increased rapidly, and their summons to follow them often have become best-sellers, such as T. Merton's book and a few others.

This method of attaining idealistic or ideational reintegration of culture is very easy. It is accessible to almost everyone: hence its mass popularity. On the other hand, it is not very creative. It merely accepts previously created systems without re-creating them in an important way and insofar it is a form of sociocultural stagnation rather than of a creative growth. It may serve as a stop-gap before a new system is created; but it cannot be the genuine method of re-creating and reintegrating a culture.

Somewhat approximating this method is that part of the majority who, like the Neo-Thomists, the Neo-Neo-Platonists, the Neo-Neo-Sufis, the Neo-Neo-Confucianists, or the Neo-Neo-Vedantists, modify this or that part of their system of the past. Their innovations are so modest, however, that they amount to little and cannot solve the problem of a creative reintegration of culture.

So far, only a small minority has achieved this task through a genuine creative effort in various fields of culture. After a critical examination of the treasury of humanity's values some people try to separate perennial and universal values from temporary and local ones, and great values from pseudo-values; and then they attempt to create a new system of values that incorporates only the real, the immortal, and the noblest values of truth, goodness, and beauty, which can serve the whole of humanity. Efforts of that sort have not yet produced any new great cultural system, but they have supplied some elements toward a solution of the problem.

In this spirit some scientists and inventors conscientiously work only on constructive discoveries and inventions, for the benefit of humanity and the greater glory of God, refusing to work upon destructive devices. Similarly some artists, poets, writers, painters, sculptors, architects, composers, musicians, and actors refuse to lend themselves to any further prostitution of the fine arts for the sake of market, personal profit, or popularity and fame, sincerely striving to create only what is really beautiful, and at the same time true and good, as any real beauty is. Their efforts have not yet produced any great masterpiece, but small contributions to that end are increasing.

The only field in which the notable creators of integralist values have already appeared is the field of goodness — the field of culture where creative reintegration is especially needed. Eminent leaders such as Gandhi, Schweitzer, Sri Aurobindo, and a host of less well known but equally great apostles of goodness — the Friends, thousands of "good neighbors" who unselfishly serve others — these furnish examples of the creators of goodness. Their ethics in theory and practice is indeed a truly creative variation of the great systems of integralist ethics. Since the field of sensate ethics and moral conduct has disintegrated, the need of reintegration there is especially urgent at the present time. It is fortunate, therefore, that these geniuses of goodness have already appeared in this field. They already show the pattern, the way, and the technique which will produce a true integralist reintegration of moral values.

To sum up: although a creative reintegration of our culture along integralist lines is still in its first stage, there is no doubt that it will rapidly develop if the madness of sensate disintegration does not lead humanity to suicide.

Such, in brief, are the main trends, disintegrations, polarizations, and reintegrations of Western man, society, and culture that evolved during the last decade or so. Their total spectrum is still somber and threatening; but it is not hopeless. If mankind does not destroy itself in the next few decades, the disintegration of sensate culture will be completed and a creative reintegration will emerge. In this way the crisis of our age will be ended, and a new creative era will open up in the life of humanity.

CHAPTER FIVE

Totalitarianism: Its Causes and Fluctuations

1. THE LAW OF THE FLUCTUATION OF GOVERNMENT REGIMENTATION

Listening to the heated debate between the partisans of a mild or strong totalitarianism like the New Dealers, the Fair Dealers, the Fascists, the Nazis, various socialists and Communists on one hand, and the glorifiers of capitalism, democracy, and free enterprise on the other, one is struck by the wholesale ignorance of the debaters about the topic of their debate. Still greater seems to be the ignorance of those who, at the present time, advocate and condone "surgical operation" in the form of a gigantic military armament and preparation for war, for an extermination of Communist and other forms of totalitarianism. Both parties apparently regard the rise and decline of totalitarianism as something caused merely by the arbitrary wishes of the ruling groups, as something depending entirely upon the wisdom or folly of this or that government. As to the partisans of the surgical extermination of Communist totalitarianism, they evidently are unaware that exactly this surgical operation of theirs is the best fertilizer for a particularly strong growth of totalitarianism in its Communist, Fascist, Nazi, or simply military variety. These partisans evidently do not realize that the objective consequences of their actions tend to kill freedom, democracy, and free enterprise, and build totalitarianism.

143

The reason for this is the well-ascertained causal law that totalitarianism of any kind is generated and nursed by an important social emergency. *As soon as any important emergency or calamity occurs in a given society, the control and regimentation of its government begins to expand and grow; as soon as the emergency subsides, the government control declines.* War is one of the greatest emergencies; as such, war always tends to breed totalitarianism. Peace is lack of war emergency. Therefore it generates quantitative and qualitative decline of governmental regimentation, and breeds freedom, democracy, and free enterprise. Let us look at the matter more closely:

The main uniform effect of calamities upon the political, economic, and social structure of society consists of an expansion of governmental regimentation and control of behavior and social relationships of the individuals and groups, or, in a decrease of their self-control and self-management in the field of their behavior and relationships. The expansion of governmental control assumes a variety of forms. Now it takes the form of Communist or socialist totalitarianism; now that of Nazi or Fascist, monarchical or simply military totalitarianism. Their colors and details, the bosses and the victims vary; but their essence — an abnormally expanded coercive government regulation of the behavior and relationships of the citizens — is similar, often identical in all these varieties of totalitarianism. Now it is effected by a revolutionary regime, now by a counter-revolutionary regime; now by a dictatorial bureaucracy, now by a military dictatorship; now by captains of industry, now by labor rulers. From both the quantitative and the qualitative points of view, such an expansion of governmental control means a decrease of freedom of individuals and private groups and a decline of truly democratic institutions.

If the calamity is slight and short-lived, its political and social repercussions are correspondingly slight and short-lived. If, on the contrary, it is acute and of long duration, the totalitarian, auto-cratic, or dictatorial trend assumes a more drastic and less ephe-meral character.

An increase of totalitarianism manifests itself first in those fields of social relationships in which the calamity creates the gravest emergency. In case of famine or great business depres-sion, governmental regimentation is applied first of all to the field of food supply and economic relationships, embracing do-mestic production, distribution, and consumption, exportation and importation, rationing, price control, and so on. In an effort to regulate the economic factors, governmental regimen-tation extends over almost the entire economic life of the nation, and frequently comprises, as well, a number of non-economic relationships.

In the event of pestilence, governmental control increases first of all in the field of health, prescribing certain sanitary and quarantine measures and prohibiting certain forms of behavior.

If the calamity is complex, and involves famine, pestilence, revolution, and war, then the increase of dictatorship and regimentation becomes fairly encyclopedic, extending to prac-tically all fields of social relationships. The population either strictly obeys orders or else is thrown into prison or concentration camps or consigned to the guillotine, the gallows, or a firing squad.

Totalitarianism masquerades under a variety of slogans and shibboleths, such as government "by the grace of God," "by the people," "by the proletariat," and "by the will of the Revolu-tion," all of which constitute merely a smoke screen designed to conceal the basic despotism and autocracy whereby the liberties and inalienable rights of the citizenry are trampled under foot. This elemental truth seems not to have been gen-erally apprehended, in spite of the fact that it has been re-peatedly stressed by social thinkers from Lao Tse, Confucius,

Mencius, Plato, Aristotle, and St. Augustine up to Le Play and Herbert Spencer.[1] The only essential difference between various totalitarianisms is that one is coercively imposed upon the citizens whereas another is claimed to be willingly accepted by them. Moreover, it is hard to decide which is mainly compulsory and which, for the most part, is voluntarily accepted. One has hardly any solid ground, for instance, for the argument that the totalitarianism of Sparta or ancient Egypt was more compulsory than that of Stalin or Hitler or even of the war cabinets of modern democracies.

Finally, the transformation of the regime in response to major catastrophes depends very little upon the personnel. No matter who is at the helm, and no matter how strongly the leaders may dislike totalitarianism, an expansion of governmental regimentation is as inevitable as the rise of temperature in influenza or pneumonia; otherwise the particular incumbents will be ousted from office and replaced by more amenable officials. If the existing government is wise and competent, it will perform the necessary social operations like a first-class surgeon — skillfully and with a minimum of pain and bloodshed. If it is stupid and incompetent, it will perform the operation with the clumsiness of a butcher, imposing unnecessary physical, economic, social, and mental hardships upon the population. Totalitarianism is not created by Pharaohs, monarchs, and dictators. The Lenins, Stalins, Mussolinis, Hitlers, and other Führers are merely the instruments of deeper underlying forces that decree an increase of totalitarianism during signal calamities.

When the emergency is over, the *opposite* trend uniformly sets in — a *decrease* of governmental regimentation. If at that time the same Stalins and Hitlers, Diocletians or Suleimans are in

---

[1] This lack of understanding is clearly evidenced in the Second World War, with its slogan "democracy vs. totalitarianism"; for Stalin's regime was even more totalitarian than Hitler's, and the war governments of the "democracies" had become about as totalitarian as those of the Axis powers.

the saddle, either they themselves effect this change, or they are ousted from control of the state. *This uniformity is one of the most fundamental among all the uniformities in the field of social and political phenomena.*

Let us now undertake a concise inductive verification of these propositions based upon daily observations and relevant historical facts.

2. The Specific Increase of Totalitarianism in Response to Sundry Calamities

By daily observation we know that at the cross sections of streets and other places with enormous traffic, there usually are policemen controlling the traffic in an obligatory way. On the highways and the streets with no traffic emergency, there is no regular traffic policeman, and no governmental regimentation of the movement of the cars. When an emergency, say an accident, however, occurs at such places, the policemen and their obligatory regimentation regularly appear. And the greater the traffic emergency, the greater the number of traffic cops and the amount of their regimentation.

Daily observation shows further that as soon as a fire breaks out in a building of a city, police, side by side with the fire brigade, regularly appear and begin to regiment the behavior of the people there.

When there is no scarcity (or emergency) of air, no government tries to regulate its use. When a scarcity (or emergency) of air appears — in radio network, television, or air-transportation — obligatory legislation and its enforcement regularly emerge.

There are other daily situations where the discussed law of increase and decrease of governmental regimentation as caused by an emergency or its lack can be daily observed. Countless numbers of such reoccurrences well corroborate the given causal formula of totalitarianism.

In response to the impact of war, pestilence, floods, earthquakes, devastating explosions or fires, and similar catastrophes, more rigid governmental control at once takes place in the form of martial, siege, and other emergency laws. Private property (such as cars and boats) is requisitioned, curfew and sanitary measures are introduced, part of the population is evacuated, and penalties for the violation of the prescribed orders become more drastic. The sequel of the terrific Halifax explosion, which occurred during the First World War (December 6, 1917), presents a concrete example of the general uniformity. Immediately after the disaster the lieutenant governor sent to the chief of police of Halifax the following order: "You are hereby authorized to commandeer and make use of any vehicle of any kind that you find necessary for the purpose of removing the injured and the dead of this city."

"Military orders to vacate the North End district followed hard upon the explosion. [Almost at once] the military established a cordon around the devastated district, which no one was allowed to pass without an order."[2]

Various authorities busied themselves with the work of relief and rehabilitation. Legislative acts were passed conferring discretionary power to expropriate property, to repair or reconstruct buildings, to amend or repeal provisions of the city charter and the workmen's compensation act, etc.

The above enumeration indicates that the government extended its authority to cover economic interests, including the rights of private property and those of the working classes; freedom of traffic; and many other basic interests and activities which had hitherto enjoyed a large measure of freedom from governmental control.

This expansion of governmental regulation was perhaps even

---

2 See S. H. Prince's *Catastrophe and Social Changes* (New York, 1920), pp. 100 ff.

more conspicuous in the case of the great Chicago fire and the San Francisco earthquake or other sudden calamities.

A. The Increase of Governmental Regulation in Pestilence. Upon the outbreak of a grave pestilence the government of the respective city, town, or country has almost invariably issued regulations extending its control to many social relationships hitherto unregimented by it. In some cities it has instituted quarantine measures prohibiting entrance into the areas affected, restricting the burial of the dead to certain places and hours, isolating all who were in contact with the sick from any contact with others, and forbidding the occupants of the infected regions to move to other districts. These regulations have been implemented by drastic penalties, including the confiscation of property and even capital punishment. In Rouen, during the plague of 1507, the government decreed that "everything is to be eliminated that could arouse the anger of God, such as gambling, cursing, drinking and all excesses." In Speyer and Tournai an edict ordered the expulsion or marriage of all concubines, the rigorous observance of Sunday, the elimination of dice games and of gambling in general, the expulsion of drunkards, beggars, lepers, and gypsies, etc.[3] These measures frequently extended far beyond the ordinary sanitary, ethical, and religious regulations. In China, in the famines and plagues of 1313-1318, 1324, 1333, etc., the government "abolished the Buddhist priesthood as the cause of all misfortunes," restrained the taxgatherers in the districts affected, and regimented the distribution of grain.[4]

In England, during the famine and pestilence of 1269, citizens were forbidden to leave London, to buy food in the outside markets, or to debase the coinage. The government fixed the

---

[3] See J. Nohl, *The Black Death,* tr. by C. H. Clarke (London, 1926), pp. 108 ff.

[4] Charles Creighton, *History of Epidemics in England* (Cambridge, 1891), I, 151-152.

prices of commodities, prohibiting extravagant housekeeping, and so on.[5]

In the plague of 1349 a royal proclamation of December first ordered the authorities "to stop the passage beyond sea of them that have no mandate." A proclamation of 1350 decreed that all persons under sixty, "not living by a trade or handicraft, not possessing private means, nor having land to cultivate, shall be obliged, when required, to serve any master who is willing to hire him or her at such wages as were usually paid in the locality in the year 1346," and prohibited laborers from leaving their manor.[6] With a slight variation this "story" is continued up to this day. As soon as a serious epidemic arises, the government invariably introduces many regulations of the relationships hitherto not governmentally regimented.

B. The Increase of Government Control in Famine and Economic Emergency. In this field the expansion of government interference and the shift of the political regime toward totalitarianism are still more conspicuous than in the case of pestilence. As in other calamities, this shift may take place peacefully, the existing government itself effecting the change, or it may assume a violent form, the existing regime, incapable of carrying out the process, being replaced by a revolutionary regime. *Other conditions being equal, the greater the contrast between the rich and the poor, the sharper the increase of governmental regulation.*

An increase of governmental economic control during periods of famine or impoverishment has regularly manifested itself in the following phenomena: first, in an establishment or reinforcement of governmental control of exports and imports, which has often amounted to a government monopoly of foreign

---

[5] *Ibid.,* pp. 49-50.
[6] *Ibid.,* pp. 180 ff.

trade; second, in an establishment of fixed prices for food and other necessities; third, in registration and tabulation of the total volume of necessities in the country owned by its citizens; fourth, in a complete control of the purchase and sale of commodities, including the amounts to be bought; fifth, in the requirement that private citizens send their commodities to market; sixth, in the requisition, to an extraordinary degree, of private necessities; seventh, in the establishment of numerous governmental agencies for the purpose of buying, producing, and distributing necessities among the population; eighth, in the introduction of a ration system; ninth, in an organization of public works on an extraordinarily large scale.

This expansion of governmental control has sometimes amounted to almost complete totalitarianism, in its Communistic, socialistic, state-socialist, fascist, or other forms. The following data offer a few typical instances of the phenomenon.

Ancient Egypt. The Bible gives us one of the oldest records which clearly show the foregoing correlation. As a result of the great famine in the time of Joseph, the money, cattle, and land of the population of ancient Egypt "became Pharaoh's." The people became the "slaves" of the government. The entire economic life began to be controlled by the government. In modern terminology this means that everything was nationalized.[7] Other Egyptian records show that this was repeated several times in the history of ancient Egypt. Its pharaohs and officials often stress in their records the fact that "in years of famine they plowed all the fields of the nome, preserving its people alive and furnishing its food."[8] The frequence of war and famine or the danger of famine in ancient Egypt accounts for the perennially high level of government control. And in the famine

---

[7] See Genesis 47:13-20.

[8] J. H. Breasted, *Ancient Records of Egypt,* Vol. I, sects. 189, 281, 459, 523, *et al.*

years and in periods of impoverishment this control seems to have become even more rigorous. Thus in Egypt under the Ptolemies, the economic disorganization of Egypt was accompanied by an extraordinary growth of governmental control which led to a transformation of Egyptian society into a universal state-socialist, or totalitarian, organization.[9]

China. More abundant and conspicuous confirmation of the hypothesis is furnished by the history of China. It is the history of a society with very frequent famines and with permanent danger of starvation. This accounts for the uniquely high level of governmental control in China throughout its history. The organization of Chinese society has been in essence "an economic state socialism," with "many governmental regulations to control consumption, production, and distribution."[10] And in periods of acute famine or impoverishment, governmental control expanded still further. This, according to the records, invariably happened in the time of the Yao, and in the years of famine during the rule of the Yin, the Chow, the Han, the Tang, the Sung, and other dynasties. Moreover, the attempts to introduce a real state-socialist or totalitarian organization, such as those of Wang Mang or Wang an Shih, regularly took place in periods of grave impoverishment.[11]

Ancient Greece. Aside from the factor of militarism, economic insecurity was responsible for a large degree of governmental control in Sparta, Athens, Lipara, and other Greek states. Pohlmann says: "The products of the Spartan agriculture were not sufficient to satisfy the needs of the population. The entire eco-

---

[9] Cf. M. Rostovtzeff's *State and Personality in the Economic Life of the Ptolemaic Egypt* (Russian, *Sovremennya Zapiski*), No. 10; also his *Social and Economic History of the Hellenistic World*, I, 267 ff.

[10] Chen Huan Chang, *The Economic Principles of Confucius,* Columbia University Studies, Vol. XLIV (1911), No. I, pp. 168 ff.; No. II, pp. 497 ff.

[11] Cf. Mabel P. H. Lee's *The Economic History of China* (New York, 1921), pp. 40, 46, 58-60, 63, 77-80, 83, 92, 99, 101-104, 110, 122, 140, 155, *et passim.*

nomic life rested on a very narrow and uncertain basis. Every economic crisis, every delay or interruption in the importation of necessities, was very dangerous. Is it any wonder that the most rigorous governmental control of economic life became inevitable?" [12] In similar straits was Athens. [13] Attica consumed 3,400,000 medimni of bread, while it produced at most only 2,400,000. In case of a poor crop the danger of famine grew serious.

"As soon as the prices of necessities began to go up, state interference took on unprecedented forms. To cope with the coming famine the state organized an extraordinary commission of Sitons with unlimited control over economic life." Often the private control of economic relations was almost completely superseded by that of the government, in the production and distribution of necessities and in the field of economic life in general. [14] In the periods of extreme impoverishment, governmental control assumed the forms of the Russian Communism of 1918-1920. The government confiscated private lands and wealth, distributed them in such a way as it found necessary, nationalized what it wanted — in brief, pushed its control to the maximum limit. Such were, for example, the periods of impoverishment after the Messina War, and in the times of Agis IV, Cleomenes III, and Nabis in Sparta, and after the Peloponnesian War in Athens (the periods of the Thirty Tyrants and the Ten Tyrants). Either in a legal way or in the form of revolution, under conservative as well as revolutionary dictators,

---

[12] R. Pohlmann, *Geschichte des antiken Communismus und Sozialismus* (Russian translation), pp. 32 ff,, 430 ff.

[13] Cf. A. Bockh's *Die Staatshaushaltung der Athener I* (Berlin, 1851), pp. 125 ff., and Novosadsky's "The Struggle Against Dearth in Ancient Greece," *The Journal of the Ministry of Public Education* (Russian), 1917, pp. 78-80.

[14] Novosadsky, *op. cit.*, pp. 80-82; Pohlmann, *op. cit.*, pp. 235-236; Bockh, *op. cit.*, pp. 116-125; Francotte, "Le Pain à Bon Marché et le Pain Gratuit dans les Cités Grecques," in *Mélanges du Droit public Grec* (Paris, 1910), pp. 291 ff.

state interference in such periods attained its utmost limit and assumed the form of state socialism or totalitarianism.[15]

Ancient Rome. A similar parallelism is seen in the history of Rome. Here the years of famine, such as the years 5, 8, 18, and 52 A.D., were usually marked by a corresponding increase of governmental control. Side by side with these small fluctuations we note that the periods of impoverishment of the masses were followed by an expansion of state interference which amounted sometimes to state socialism or totalitarianism. It is well known that the period from the second half of the second century B.C. to the beginning of the first century A.D. was one of striking economic disorganization. The same period is marked by the Corn Laws of the Gracchi (123 B.C.); by the establishment of a special institution for the prevention of famine and for control of a public supply (104 B.C. — in Caesar's time it became permanent; in the famine of 22 B.C. Augustus became its head [*curator annonae*]); by the introduction of a rationing system and public supply free of charge; by many acts of nationalization, confiscation, and restriction of private economic enterprise; and by a huge increase in the general economic functions of the government.[16] The apparatus for this ever-expanding control of economic life grew into a colossal mechanism served by an enormous number of agents who requisitioned, bought, transported, weighed, and stored commodities. Private business in this field was reduced virtually to zero. The number of the

---

[15] Cf. P. Giraud's *Etudes économiques sur l'antiquité* (Paris, 1905), pp. 68 ff.; G. Buzold's *Griechische Geschichte* (Gotha, 1902-1903), Teil III, pp. 1456, 1614, 1628; B. Niese, *Geschichte der Griechischen und Macedonischen Staaten* (Gotha, 1893-1903), Teil II, pp. 296 ff. and Teil III, pp. 42 ff.; M. Rostovtzeff's *Social and Economic History of the Hellenistic World*, pp. 208 ff.; and W. W. Tarn's *The Hellenistic Age* (Cambridge, 1925).

[16] Cf. O. Hirschfeld's *Die kaiserlichen Verwaltungsbeamten* (Berlin, 1905), pp. 231 ff.; J. P. Waltzing's *Etude historique sur les Corporations Professionelles chez les Romains* (Louvain, 1896), I, 26-103; and M. Rostovtzeff's *The Roman Leaden Tessera* (Russian), 1903, pp. 111-113, and his *Social and Economic History of the Roman Empire*.

proletariat supplied with free rations steadily grew, amounting in the time of Julius Caesar to some 600,000 in Rome alone. Besides bread the rationing system eventually came to include oil, pork, wine, clothing, admission to theaters, and even special ration cards for prostitutes (*lasciva nomismata*) which entitled the bearer to the services of one of the Roman prostitutes.

Still more conspicuous was the correlation during the period from the third century A.D. to the fall of the Western Roman Empire. This was a time of economic decay. It also witnessed the establishment of a state-socialistic economic organization in the Western Roman Empire. "The Empire was transformed into a big factory where, under the control of the officials, the population was forced to work. . . . Almost all production and distribution of wealth was concentrated in the hands of the government."[17] In brief, it was a full-fledged totalitarian regime. One who has observed the Soviet Communist system in the period from 1917 to 1922 is struck by the essential similarity of the Roman and Soviet regimes.

The Middle Ages. Here the same correlation is repeated many times. Charlemagne introduced fixed prices under famine conditions (those of 792-793). In the famine of 805 a decree was issued that *"ne foris imperium nostrum vendatur aliquid alimoniae"*; freedom of contract was restricted; free trade was forbidden; fixed prices were reintroduced; agriculture and industry began to be controlled more severely, and so forth.[18] As famine was very frequent in the Middle Ages, this factor, besides the factor of war, seems to have been responsible for a relatively high degree of government control of economic relations. In famine years this rose still higher. In the history of England

---

[17] J. P. Waltzing, *op. cit.*, II, 383-384; Duruy, *Histoire des Romains* (1885), VIII 550 ff.

[18] F. Curschmann, *Hungersnöte im Mittelalter* (Leipzig, 1944), pp. 71-75, *et passim.*

such years were 1201-1202, 1315-1316, 1321, 1483, 1512, 1521, 1586, and 1648-1649. In the history of France such years were 1391, 1504-1505, 1565, 1567, 1577, 1591, 1635, 1662, 1684, 1693, and 1709. A historian of the food trade in France sums up his exhaustive study as follows: "As soon as famine broke out, governmental control grew stronger; as soon as it declined, this control weakened."[19]

The correlation is still more conspicuously exhibited in the history of Russian famines. Those of 1279, 1452, 1601-1603, 1674, 1682, 1723, 1734, 1798-1802, 1805-1806, 1812, 1839, 1848, 1854-1855, 1891-1892, 1905-1906, and 1918-1922 were invariably attended by government control of all exports and imports; the establishment of fixed prices for commodities; direct and indirect rationing of food and other commodities; a search for hoarded stocks; the distribution of free food; compulsory collective and communistic agricultural projects; the systematic curtailment of private business; a sort of W.P.A. and C.C.C. civilian army, controlled by the state and used for the execution of state projects; and outright totalitarianism during the major famines reinforced by pestilence, war, and revolution, such as the acute crises of 1601-1603 and 1918-1922.[20]

---

[19] G. E. Afanassieff, *The Conditions of the Food Trade* (Russian, 1892), pp. 1-3, 8, 17, 144-148, 155, 158. A. Akaskranianz, "Die Franzosische Getreidehandelspolitik bis zum Jahre 1769," *Schmollers Staats- und Sozialwissenschaftliche Forschungen* (1882), Vol. 4, pp. 3, 10-14; C. Creighton, *op. cit.*, I, 49-50, 151, 178 ff. It is curious to note that the phenomenon in question regularly occurred even when the heads of the French government were inimical to an expansion of governmental control of economic affairs. An example is given by Turgot. In 1774, he decreed complete freedom of trade. In 1775, under the influence of the famine of 1774-1775, he was forced to annul his decree. The same happened with Necker, Du Pont de Nemours, and the National Assembly (see Afanassieff, *op. cit.*, pp. 299 ff., 370-371). All these governments decreed free trade in food supplies (cf. the National Assembly's edicts of 1789, 1790, and 1791). Yet all these laws remained impotent: owing to the increase of famine and poverty, governmental control grew until in the Jacobin dictatorship it became fully totalitarian.

[20] Cf. P. Sorokin's "The Influence of Famine upon Social Organization," *Russian Economist* (in Russian) 1922, No. 2.

Finally, a striking confirmation of all the hypotheses is afforded by the expansion of governmental control during and after the First and Second World Wars. During the wars, not only in the belligerent but in the neutral countries as well, the control of economic life by the governments increased enormously. In the belligerent countries it was due primarily to the factor of war, and only secondarily to that of the scarcity of food and other necessities. After the armistice in 1918, the government control of economic relationships somewhat subsided in those countries which were peaceful internally and improved economically. In the countries troubled by civil war, famine, pestilence and other calamities, the factor of poverty in conjunction with those of war and revolution, was also instrumental in generating the extreme forms of Communist totalitarianism in Russia and the Nazi and Fascist totalitarianisms in other countries in the postwar years and especially after the onset of the depression of 1929. These decades have been distinguished in virtually all Western countries by a highly developed government control over both economic and non-economic activities. Where only the depression or the famine factor has been operative, the swing toward totalitarianism has been moderate, but where these factors have been reinforced by war and revolution, the trend has assumed catastrophic proportions, leading in Russia, Italy, Germany, Hungary, Greece, and elsewhere to extreme totalitarian regimes of the Communistic, socialistic, fascistic, or military type. Private property has been either abolished or drastically curtailed, and the same has been true of private business.

Finally, even in the so-called *anti*-totalitarian or democratic countries, such as Great Britain and the United States (especially after 1929), the impoverishment due to the great depression has produced an increase of regimentation. In spite of his personal antipathy toward governmental regulation, President Hoover (like Turgot in France in 1775) after the crash of 1929 extended federal control to many areas of economic life hitherto left to private persons or groups. As the depression deepened during the subsequent years, the process went still further under the Roosevelt administration and the New Deal. It is to be noted that the forces responsible for the phenomenon have not been personal predilections of the particular administration, but rather the vastly deeper forces released by the depression. The measures adopted were merely a repetition of those taken by ancient Egypt, ancient China, India, Greece, or Rome, or any other country under like circumstances. As a matter of fact, in all the measures of the New Deal there is scarcely one that does not find its prototype in the expedients invented in the remote past for coping with similar emergencies. Finally, the same story in the most conspicuous form has been repeated in the scarcity years of the Second World War and those of the Korean police action.

C. *The Increase of Government Control in War.* Herbert Spencer showed convincingly that war causes an expansion of government control and a change of the political regime in the direction of the "militant," or (in our own terminology) the totalitarian, system.[21] His induction is well corroborated by the historical facts. The reasons for such a mutation of the sociopolitical system in time of war are rather evident. In the first place, the organization of any efficient army or navy makes it a clear-cut totalitarian institution. The soldiers live in quarters not of their own choosing; they eat what is set before them; they wear prescribed uniforms; and from reveille until taps all their activities (save when they are on furlough) are severely regimented. Furthermore, the commanding officer is an autocrat, obedience

---

[21] Cf. Herbert Spencer's *Principles of Sociology* (New York, 1910), Vol. II, chaps. 17, 18; also W. G. Sumner's *War and Other Essays* (New Haven, 1911), and R. Pohlmann, *op. cit.*

to whose legitimate orders is obligatory. The commander-in-chief is entitled to send thousands to die. In a word, any good army is a totalitarian organization par excellence. As such, and because of its paramount importance in time of war, it naturally influences the whole civil population and the government regime in the trend toward totalitarianism. It becomes the most important school for the inculcation of discipline, centralization, bureaucracy, and autocratic control.

Again, as Spencer rightly remarked, in time of war centralized and autocratic control of the civil population is a necessity. Victory is more likely to be achieved by a country which constitutes a centralized machine, with the government regimenting the population, its activities and resources, in much the same way as the military authorities rule a well-disciplined army. A nation whose citizens in time of war debate the question whether to fight or not to fight, to obey or not to obey the decrees of the government, to sacrifice or not to sacrifice, such a nation would certainly suffer defeat at the hands of the enemy. As victory and defeat are often a question of life and death for the societies involved, large-scale wars have always led to a militarization or totalitarianization of the belligerent society in its social, economic, and political organization.

War regularly results in a replacement of the normal laws by martial, siege, or emergency laws, which means an enormous increase of the area and rigidity of government control. It likewise leads frequently to a substitution of military rule for the normal city government — another form of the totalitarian movement. Again, it may lead to the establishment of a dictatorship, in the sense of the old Roman dictatorship, or of a government unlimited by any constitutional restraints. This again represents merely a variety of totalitarianism. War often requires the conscription not only of the man power of the country but of all its resources, including private property. The limitation of property rights; the expansion of government in the field of business at the expense of private business; the replacement, by the government, of private individuals and groups in the production, distribution, and consumption of commodities: such measures are concomitants of practically every strenuous war between complex societies. The complete (factual or juridical) elimination of private property is another phenomenon repeatedly associated with major conflicts, constituting a special case of the loss of constitutional and other civil liberties, which in time of war are usually either greatly restricted or else suspended altogether.

The foregoing reasons are sufficient to explain why the sociopolitical constitution of a belligerent society invariably changes in the direction of totalitarianism.

They explain, as well, why nations that have been most frequently involved in strenuous wars exhibit even in normal times a sociopolitical regime much more totalitarian than that of the more peaceful societies. So long as the vast expanses of the Pacific and the Atlantic oceans rendered the United States relatively safe from invasion, it could afford to be — and was — much less totalitarian than many European or other nations. When these oceans ceased to constitute serious obstacles to invasion, the United States was forced not merely to expand its army but also to change its sociopolitical organization in the direction of the expansion of government control — the regimentation of industry, business, and civil activities in general.

The ideologies and speech reactions that justify such transformations differ: the totalitarian trend is covered now by "Communist" ideology; now by a Nazi "philosophy," now by "democracy," "liberal," "national," and other ideologies. The alleged motive is to defend religion, or to carry the banners of civilization and progress to the "infidels" or "barbarians," or something else. But in spite of the disparity of the ideologies and slogans, the central phenomenon in all wars remains essentially constant — that is, a shift toward totalitarianism.

A careful corroboration of the proposition by the facts of history makes it one of the strongest inductive uniformities. Its validity is well demonstrated by the history of ancient Egypt, Babylonia, Iran, Greece, and Rome, as well as by that of India, China and Japan, Byzantium, the Mohammedan world, the Inca empire, medieval and modern Europe, and America. *Those countries which were more belligerent were more totalitarian in their social, economic, and political organization than those which were less belligerent,* as is notably illustrated, among the states of ancient Greece, by the contrasting regimes of Sparta and Athens.

The enormous upswing of governmental control during the World Wars and also in the present conflict offers a further illustration of the general rule. With the outbreak of the First World War all the belligerent countries became to a considerable degree totalitarian, whether they were republics or monarchies, autocracies or democracies. The capitalist economy was replaced by *Zwangsökonomie,* or *Zwangswirtschaft* — that is, by a coercive governmental economy. Private business was substantially replaced by business run by the government. Private property and wealth were increasingly limited through conscription, requisition, confiscation, "nationalization," "socialization," and the like. This process set in long before the Communist or Fascist regimes came upon the scene. In Russia the Rubicon that separated the capitalist and private-property regimes from those of the Communist or Fascist type had already been crossed by 1915, when the Czarist government (on August 17 and 25) issued decrees entitling it to search for food supplies in any private concern, to requisition or confiscate anything necessary, to check and verify the business records of any private concern, to take any enterprise under government management, etc. The totalitarian system was already born in 1915. The rest was a mere extension of it through further totalitarian measures on the part of the Czarist government, then the Kerensky government, and finally the Communist government. The last named, in a modified form and under different slogans, continued the totalitarian trend of the preceding regimes and carried it to its extreme limit. From this standpoint, Communism was not initiated by Lenin, Trotsky, or Stalin. The most they did was to perform a necessary social operation. Unfortunately they did it in the most incompetent, bloody, cruel, and destructive way, under the guidance of their "Communist ideology."

Such an extreme form of the totalitarian trend was not caused by a single factor, but rather by the concurrence of several major calamities: namely, famine, pestilence, war, and revolution. Since each of these calamities in itself tends to produce totalitarianism, it is obvious that their unholy alliance was bound to boost governmental control in Communist Russia to its uttermost limit. The life of every individual was completely regimented, the regime prescribing what, when, and where he should eat or drink, what he should wear, where he should live, and what he should read, say, believe. The "citizens" became mere puppets whose strings were pulled by the Communist government.

The subsequent story is likewise instructive. By 1921 the civil war was virtually over. The factor of international war and in large part that of revolution had ceased to operate. The curve of governmental interference accordingly began to decline. The "New Economic Policy" was introduced, which means a decrease of government control in the economic and other fields, and a corresponding growth of private autonomy. Toward 1929 the clouds of war began to gather once more on the horizon; at the same time, famine again reared its ugly head, assuming in many regions acute intensity. The preparations for the coming war commenced to eat up the greater part of the national wealth and income: hence a new upsurge of totalitarianism in 1929 and the following years. By 1935 or 1936, however, economic conditions had considerably improved; the revolution as such was dead; the new regime had become firmly rooted; and the preparations for war were deemed to have gone far enough. The result was a de-Communization of the Stalin regime, which increasingly assumed the essential characteristics of the old regime. Many values, such as the family, and Russian poetry, literature, music, and fine arts—with their Pushkins and Dostoevskis, Tchaikovskys and Lomonosoffs — were now enthroned again, sometimes on an even higher plane than had been the case during the old regime. Abortions were prohibited and divorces limited. Chastity and virginity began to be praised in the editorials of *Izvestia* and *Pravda*. Marxian textbooks of Russian history were destroyed, being replaced by texts that eulogized the great generals, emperors, statesmen and builders of the old Russia. Religion and similar values ceased to be sharply persecuted. Individual economic interests were recognized and began to be remunerated; and the privilege of individual possession or lease of real property up to ninety-nine years was introduced.

But with the outbreak of the Second World War and the Russo-Finnish War the pendulum started to swing in the opposite direction once more. Government control flared up again in an extreme form, though the ideologies and slogans that were now employed were very different from those of earlier years. Their place was taken by a nationalistic and patriotic ideology stressing the defense of the "Soviet Fatherland," and the liberties of the people against foreign aggression.

In other belligerent countries also there was a sharp upswing of governmental regimentation after the declaration of the First World War, and a notable decline after its close. With the onset of the depression at the end of the nineteen-twenties, an upward trend again set in. In Germany, Italy, Hungary, and elsewhere, where the economic situation was that of the "have-nots," the increase was much more accentuated, and eventually led to the emergence of Fascist and Nazi totalitarianisms, a form not so extreme as the Russian brand, but extreme enough in comparison with the normal regimes of the respective countries.

Since the outbreak of the Second World War the curve of government control rose so sharply in all fighting countries that the capitalistic system that prevailed prior to 1914 now appears as a relic of the remote past. Its place has been taken by a "planned" or "war" economy managed principally by the government. Private property and private business have rapidly gone into the discard. Constitutional guarantees have been progressively set aside even in the democracies. With the entrance of the United States into the war, the greater part of our industry and finance began to be managed by Washington. Most factories were producing what they had been ordered to produce, and were operating under the direct or indirect control of the federal government. As to consumer goods, the following list of articles were either "frozen" or rationed almost immediately after the United States entered the war:

Jan. 5, 1941 — new tires
Feb. 23 — recapped tires for trucks
March 2 — new automobiles
April 13 — new and used typewriters
May 4 — sugar

The following items were limited in production or delivery: gasoline and fuel oils; straight and safety razors and razor blades; metal cosmetic tubes; steel desks; paper clips.

Production was ordered stopped on these household electrical appliances:

April 22, 1941 — radios and phonographs
April 30 — refrigerators

May 31 — toasters, waffle irons, flatirons, roasters, grills, percolators, cigarette lighters, dry shavers.

March 30, 1942 — Crude rubber (banned in twenty household products and restricted in fifty others)

June 30, 1942 — lawn mowers

And so on and on, each subsequent week adding to this list. Towards the end of the Second World War the lion's share of the whole economic life of the United States was controlled by the government.

If this has happened in what is in many ways the most democratic country in the world, one can readily imagine how swift and far-reaching has been the growth of government regulation in less democratic countries!

As long as the war continued, there was no prospect of a return to the anti-totalitarian system in the field of economic, social, and political relationships. On the contrary, the totalitarian trend was bound to progress (quantitatively and qualitatively) still further, no matter who was at the helm — whether democrats, republicans, monarchists, Communists or fascists. As has been pointed out, the process does not depend upon the predilections of the party in power.

After the armistice, a partial reconversion to a less totalitarian regime started in several countries. Unfortunately, a series of revolutions, revolts, and economic emergencies have stopped this trend. These were reinforced by the dreadful emergency of the cold war, then by the Korean and other wars, then by the preparations for the Third World War. Shall we wonder that the trend towards an encyclopedic totalitarianism at its worst set forth again in all countries of the East and the West?

At the present time, all countries are feverishly reconverting towards the fully developed totalitarian regime. In the iron-curtain area, including China, totalitarianism assumed the Communist form. In Great Britain — so far — the Socialist form, which is likely to be replaced by the military-conservative form, if Churchill's party comes again to power. In the United States it is assuming the military form of MacArthur–the McCarthy–American Committee on un-American Activities–General Staff–President Truman form: a very mixed-up, peculiar American brand.

If the Third World War develops into a full-scale war, then everywhere the political, economic, and social regimes become one hundred per cent totalitarian. Their colors may differ, but their essence is going to be identical: an unlimited governmental despotism and a full suppression of all the inalienable rights and liberties of all the citizens.

D. *The Increase of Government Control in Revolution.* What has been said about war applies with still greater force to the social, economic, and political effects of revolution. During a major revolution the government is a complete dictatorship, which flouts such values as the inalienable rights of man, constitutional guarantees, the security of human life, the sacredness of private property. In superficial revolutions the expansion of governmental control is slight; in large-scale revolutions it is limitless and leads to an unrestrained extermination of those who do not support the regime, as well as to an explicit elimination of private property and to its replacement by "Communistic," "nationalized," "socialized," or, more accurately, "governmentalized" property. Such has been the case in all the outstanding revolutions of the past: the revolution in ancient Egypt of about 2500 B.C.; many Chinese revolutions (such as those at the beginning of the Christian Era and the one headed by Wang Mang); the Corcyrian revolution in Greece; the revolutions of the Ten Tyrants and the Thirty Tyrants in Athens, and those led by Agis IV, Cleomenes III, and Nabis in Sparta; a long series of other revolutions in the Hellenistic world; the Roman civil wars between Marius and Sulla, and those waged by the First and Second Triumvirate; the revolutions of the third and fourth centuries A.D.; the many medieval revolutions (such as that of the Taborites in Bohemia); the English revolution or civil war led by Cromwell (in application to the Irish and the Catholics); the French revolutions of 1789-1801 and 1871; the Russian revolutions of 1601-1603, those led by S. Rasin and Pougatcheff, and the Communist revolution of 1918; the recent Hungarian and Bavarian revolutions of 1918-1920; the Fascist and Nazi revolutions; and the legion of post-armistice revolutions, after 1945.

The extent and the concrete forms of this revolutionary totalitarianism vary. In some cases private property is not formally and explicitly abolished. Actually, however, in any notable revolution the private property of the opposing faction is subjected to requisition, confiscation, or even destruction. This applies now to the aristocracy or the rich, now to the Irish or Catholics, now to the Huguenots and other "heretics," now to the Jews, now to the "Loyalists" or "Rebels," and so forth.

Nor does a revolutionary regime show any more respect for the sanctity of human life. (Typical statistics of the number of persons executed in various revolutions are given in my *Man and Society in Calamity*, pp. 91, 185-86). Revolution is one of the most bloodthirsty and voracious monsters, devouring first the rich and the privileged, then the middle class, then many of the lower and impoverished classes, and finally the revolutionaries themselves (in the purges of one faction by another). Again, revolutionary government autocratically prescribes not only political ideas, but frequently also religious beliefs, aesthetic tastes, up to forms of love and marriage. Whoever fails to heed its mandates is likely to be handed over to a firing squad or be sent to the gallows or guillotine.

As has already been pointed out, this upsurge of totalitarian control does not depend much upon the particular leaders of the revolution or counter-revolution; for if any of them attempt to resist the inevitable trend, they are ousted from office and replaced by those who are willing to swim with the tide.[22]

The most popular revolutionary mottoes are "Liberty" and "Freedom"; yet these values are almost invariably suppressed except with reference to the revolutionary government itself and its adherents. Only after the emergency is over does the tree of liberty begin to revive and flourish again.

3. SUMMARY

Major crises generally represent a fateful concurrence of various calamities in their most acute intensity. If each of the calamities in itself promotes the growth of totalitarianism, in conjunction they push the trend to its maximum limit. Grave crises are uniformly marked by a virtually complete suppression of autonomy of individuals and groups and by unlimited governmental absolutism and despotism, interrupted, perhaps, by the overthrow of the regime by another faction, attended by a brief period of anarchy.

The phenomenon can be observed in any notable crisis, whether it be the Egyptian crises at the end of the Old, the Middle, or the New Kingdom; the severe crisis at the end of the Greco-Roman civilization and the establishment of the Christian society of the Middle Ages; the crises at the close of the Middle Ages (in the thirteenth, fourteenth, fifteenth, and sixteenth centuries); or the crisis of our own age. The foregoing analysis explains why at the present time totalitarianisms of all kinds are flourishing: why governments are absolutistic (either *de facto* or *de jure*); why the tree of civic freedom is withering; why capital-

---

[22] See for facts and evidence P. Sorokin, *Sociology of Revolution* (Philadelphia, 1925), chap. 13, *et passim; Society, Culture, and Personality* (New York, 1947), chaps. 31-33.

ism and private property are disappearing; why true democracies are becoming a mere memory. As long as the crisis lasts, there is no hope for a reversal of the trend. Only when the emergency is over (and its end does not mean merely the termination of the war) will the converse process set in.

Let the partisans of war remember this. *The medicine against Communism and totalitarianism is neither war, nor rearmament, nor threats, nor propaganda of hate, but peace, and lack of emergency.*

Index